D1264077

ALSO BY KERRY HOWLEY

Thrown

BOTTOMS UP AND THE DEVIL LAUGHS

BOTTOMS UP AND THE DEVIL LAUGHS

A JOURNEY THROUGH THE DEEP STATE

KERRY HOWLEY

ALFRED A. KNOPF, NEW YORK, 2023

THIS IS A BORZOI BOOK
PUBLISHED BY ALFRED A. KNOPF

www.aaknopf.com

Knopf, Borzoi Books, and the colophon are registered trademarks of Penguin Random House LLC.

Page 239 constitutes an extension of this copyright page.

Library of Congress Cataloging-in-Publication Data
Names: Howley, Kerry, author.
Title: Bottoms up and the devil laughs : a journey through the deep state / Kerry Howley.
Other titles: Journey through the deep state
Description: First Edition. | New York : Alfred A. Knopf, 2023. | Includes bibliographical references.
Identifiers: LCCN 2022025923 (print) | LCCN 2022025924 (ebook) | ISBN 9780525655497 (hardcover) | ISBN 9780525565048 (paperback) | ISBN 9780525655503 (ebook)
Subjects: LCSH: Official secrets—United States. | Leaks (Disclosure of information)—Political aspects—United States. | Whistle blowing—United States. | Intelligence service—United States. | United States. National Security Agency/Central Security Service. | Electronic surveillance—United States. | Drone aircraft—Government policy—United States. | Defense information, Classified—United States. | Information technology—Political aspects. | Terrorism—United States—Prevention.
Classification: LCC JF1525.S4 H69 2023 (print) | LCC JF1525.S4 (ebook) | DDC 352.3/79—dc23/eng/20220809
LC record available at https://lccn.loc.gov/2022025923
LC ebook record available at https://lccn.loc.gov/2022025924

Jacket illustration by Ben Wiseman
Jacket design by Janet Hansen

Manufactured in the United States of America

1st Printing

For Mothers of Reckless Children

Listen it's trying / to make a void again. In which to hear itself. It's too alone. Everything wants em- / bodiment. But there's this noise now it's replacing everything. This humming of agreement / fast-track skipped-step information yes yes yes yes lost hope lost will—dear dis- / embodiment, here is an old wind, watch it orchestrate event, I raise my hand to find / my face again, I know I am supposed to think I'm whole

—JORIE GRAHAM

BOTTOMS UP AND THE DEVIL LAUGHS

A NOTE ON WALLS

In the course of writing this book, in the middle of its darkest, least human chapter, I lived alone in the West Texas desert. It was a trendy town in which wealthy people had gathered, purchased homes, and abandoned them. Sometimes they had also built walls, and it was fashionable to complain about these walls. The conversation at a dinner party turned, inevitably, to the misfortune of walls built by the wealthy, which violated the expansive openness of the desert landscape. We were not far from the border, after all, where a maniac wanted to build a wall; walls were classist, racist, wrong. "They all build walls," someone said. "So ugly." "That's all recent." "Things have really changed." At which point a radiant older woman, an architect, spoke up. "That's a very protestant idea," she said. "This idea that you should be able to see inside someone else's backyard. It's an idea against ethnic clannishness." This stopped me, being both obviously correct and so contrary to the force of my thinking a moment previous. We had presumed a right to see inside each compound. We had all of us turned an aesthetic preference into a morality. Or maybe it was that we had neutered a dark kind of morality into an aesthetic preference.

Joan Didion has praised the kind of home in which "you can close the door and cry until dinner," which is to say, an architecture not so enamored by openness that it has failed to involve rooms. I kept this in mind as my husband and I were house shopping a few years ago. "Is this a house I can cry alone in?" I asked over and over. There was a house we rather liked. "But I don't know," my husband said, genuinely concerned. "Is there a room for crying?"

The morning after the desert dinner party I discovered, to my surprise, that I was pregnant. I was constructing, out of the food I had eaten at the dinner party, a wall of tough fibrous tissue around a spherical group of cells. I despaired many times, in the writing, about my ability to protect the thing I was growing from a world that had abandoned walls, that asserted its right to invade, to amass electrons against wholeness, that had forgotten what it was like to construct a self in the dark. But she is here now, in the world, and there is nothing to do but help her remember.

SURVEILLANCE IS MADE OF DOGS

Anyone can build a combat drone. If you build a drone for your little makeshift country, no one will be impressed. You could use the same engine they use for snowblowers, slap on a propeller, pour in some motor oil. We may think of drones as indestructible, ironclad, and this is the impression defense companies attempt to impart with the hard names they give machines they build: Predator drone, Reaper drone, Hunter drone; but in fact the original word, *drone,* is elegantly apt, and all of these are an attempt to mask the dumb delicacy it captures. Drones are cheap, flimsy, light little wisps of things, vulnerable to lost signals and sleepy pilots; vulnerable to gusts of wind and hard rain, lightning, ice; vulnerable even to themselves, as dropping a missile creates a thrust that threatens to spin a drone to the ground. You will send a drone whirling into the sand should you turn too hard into a breeze, or press the wrong button on your joystick; should you fly into an area of excessive electromagnetic noise or accidentally, as has happened to one American drone pilot, fly the drone upside down for a long while, oblivious. They slam into mountains, crash into other planes, fall into farms, sidewalks, waterways. Sometimes they simply go silent and float away, never to be found again. Their remains are cylinders with a wall punched out to reveal a hollow interior, as if the true drone had wormed its way out of this shell and flown on. Hundreds and hundreds of military drones we have lost this way, scattered across continents. It's okay. They're cheap. We make new ones.

What is impressive is not the drone, but the network that keeps it aloft. The satellites we rocket into the sky, bathing the globe in radio waves, invisible bouncy strands passing through you on their way back to our shallow bowled dishes, twenty feet across. We capture waves, of course, and we capture light, not only via drone, but in every way we can contrive to capture. The light and the waves come from Southeast Asia, the Middle East, Northern Africa, anywhere we can lay the hard bulk that sucks in the invisible. The waves and the light come from the United States, though much of that is technically illegal. They contain phone calls between children, YouTube tutorials, eviction notices, breakup emails, cancer diagnoses, love letters, selfies sent by text. Electrons stream through air and wire, underwater and overland. They whir back to us in search of embodiment.

On a trip with some of my dearest friends, undertaken largely but not exclusively for the reason of capturing flattering group selfies, every one of us had used up all the storage on our phones before we took a single photo. To take one selfie we had to delete, say, three. By the time we went on our next trip together, everyone had upgraded phones. Now nothing would constrain us from taking pictures, all of which still exist, somewhere, because there is no incentive to delete them.

How much of the burden is in the way we watch ourselves? In the early years of the twenty-first century, everyone is amassing digital information but no one knows how to sort through it. Closets are stacked with old computers. It would be better, of course, to go through all of one's photos and keep only those worth keeping, but the thought of this induces paralyzing exhaustion. This would involve decision-making, which is cognitively taxing. This would involve delving deep into our personal histories, our pasts, which may involve feelings we don't feel like feeling. It's best to just take another photograph. Keep building up the database. Throw it into the cloud, whatever that is. It's slightly stressful to know that one's personal database is bloated and disorganized, but you can't see my cloud. It's my burden to bear, my weight to carry; luckily, since I'm small, it's only a cloud.

In the United States in the early years of the twenty-first century, this has been the approach intelligence agencies take toward information: Absorb everything, all of it, at once. Stash it somewhere. Worry about it later.

I wanted to know what surveillance *was*. I wanted to know what it was *made of*. More data has been created and stored since the year 2000 than in the entire previous course of humanity. The NSA's upgraded phone is a giant warehouse, the size of six city blocks, sucking in water in the middle of a Utah desert. Inside are racks the size of refrigerators, and on the racks, more metal boxes, these the size of dinner plates. Inside those boxes are magnetic switches—zero one, zero one, one zero—the computer's translation of all the words it is possible to whisper. A server farm is our age's answer to the industrial factory: row upon row upon row of racks, 10,000 of them, autonomous, whirring, sucking in a small city's worth of electricity and pouring out heat. This one cost $2 billion to build; maintaining it and its generators costs millions more per year. Around it the NSA builds a fence, and on the fence they mount cameras. The sum total of human knowledge from the dawn of man to 2003 could be contained in five exabytes. The warehouse can probably hold twelve.

As you can imagine, you are not welcome on this piece of desert. But in the blueprints, one can see room for a kennel, where guard dogs must sleep, because American surveillance is partly made of electrons and partly made of tubes and partly made of dogs. The true enemy of data is not something against which dogs can protect. The enemy of all of this data, of all data, is heat. To cool the whirring racks, the NSA must pump in 1.2 million gallons of water per day, in the desert, in drought conditions. Data is physical. It can therefore be confronted.

In the early years of the twenty-first century, a Japanese woman promises to declutter our homes. She teaches us to prioritize space over things. She counsels us to clear our countertops. We throw out everything. Thrifters report that it is a glorious time to thrift; the shops are full of treasure. We take photos of our decluttered homes and save them in an increasingly anarchic digital space. The photos don't take up any room. They don't require sacrifice.

Most of us are good at not looking. Some people are very, very bad at it, which is perhaps a kind of evolutionary variance you'd want to have around. People who feel they must confront the nature of reality, whom we call "whistleblowers" or "traitors," tend to feel that the rest of us should do the same, which makes those people annoying, because *not looking* is a skill, and after a while you too might lose the ability to not look. You might feel drawn to, say, NSA Georgia, because you wanted to understand the life of someone for whom the secret had become mundane. These pages are a strange history of a world burying itself in isolated fragments, "information," data, the products of surveillance, and the twenty years in which these fragments come to be confused for fact. It is a polemic against memory cast into print.

My first real job was at a newspaper in Myanmar, which is and was a military dictatorship closed to most foreigners. I was twenty-one and never more visible; the state was watching, and so were the neighbors. The newspaper was called *The Myanmar Times and Business Review,* and it was run by a vulgar portly Australian. Before we could publish anything, we faxed what we had written to a censor, who faxed back the copy with big black *X*'s across it. You could then call the censor, whose name was Way Lin, and argue with him, at which point he would give reasons that your fluff piece on Halloween was inadmissible (ghost stories were illegal), or your profile of a rickshaw driver was axed (a driver with a degree in history suggested economic stagnation). Once, I met Way Lin at a party. He was friendly and eager to be liked. From this early experience I took a lesson in tonal complexity. What was ominous in the abstract was likely to be, in its specificities, absurd.

Being a woman is a way of being unseen, and this invisibility renders a certain confidence, a certain obliviousness to boundaries. To get to the NSA's Whitelaw Building, I needed access to Fort Gordon, an army base. I parked at a visitor's center. I explained that I was a professor doing research, which was true, and received a pass. Fort Gordon is a bleak, overgrown, dated brick affair. The architecture is sometimes brick riot-proof high school and sometimes socialist-cheap and occasionally horror-movie funhouse, as with the weathered "Bingo Palace" I passed as I circled and circled and searched for something that resembled the drawings I had seen. I felt the dirt road beneath my tires as I pulled behind some temporary buildings and passed a green scrubby field on which I may have seen some horses. There were massive satellite dishes surrounded by barbed wire. There were uniformed troops in formation. I saw nothing to contradict the idea that it was 1975. And then, in the distance, the $286 million, 604,000-square-foot Whitelaw Building, more concert hall than facility, gleaming and white and gently, expensively curved. It looked like a giant piece of consumer technology newly unwrapped. It did not look like it had been built. It looked like it had landed.

I walked up to some equally designed outdoor turnstiles, sleek metal detectors on which were posted signs: NO CELL PHONES. NO THUMB DRIVES. An SUV pulled up with a police officer inside; she demanded my license and as I handed it to her I saw her notepad read "woman in a burgundy top." I hadn't thought of it as burgundy. As I sat on a patch of grass in the sun, increasingly hot, I worried about sun damage to my face, which is to say I was thinking about wrinkles as a second SUV pulled up. They wanted my phone. I asked if I could refuse, and they said no. The police officer called these new men "special agents," though when I asked a guy for his title, he declined to say. There were two officials, then three, then six, and they were "just trying to figure out what's going on." I asked a few times if I could leave and was told I could not in fact leave; I asked if I was under arrest and was told no, this was "investigatory detention."

They asked me whether I would talk to the media and I

said I didn't know. They asked me who I was writing for and I said I didn't know, who could say where this would end up, maybe *Glimmer Train,* a literary journal. I do not know why, when stressed, my instinct is to become more annoying. "Glimmer Train," wrote the special agent on his special pad. They conferred away from me. The sun beat down and I continued to think about fine lines. "Who in the media will you speak to?" an agent asked for the third time. "I am the media," I said grandly. To my surprise, they liked this answer; it involved a definable category. I was then turned over to a third jurisdictional authority, military police. I do not know how much time all of this took. I only know that in that thirty minutes or hour or two hours something shifted, because as I sat on that patch of grass I looked not at the building but at the parking lot. I looked at the cars: Jettas and Camrys. Thousands of regular people worked here. Thousands of middle-class people drove from their homes every day and parked here and went home and never told their mothers where they'd been. The eye is not always a metaphor. Surveillance, of course, is made of us.

IMAGINARY FRIENDS

You might imagine *The Intercept,* a publication best known for publishing stuff stolen by Snowden, as an institution in which anonymous, enigmatical documents are constantly being fielded, but in fact the five printed pages that arrived in the P.O. box of *The Intercept*'s D.C. office in May 2017 struck its recipients as bizarre. No one had emailed first with an introduction and an inquiry. This was not a cultivated source, not someone who had said I work in *this* department and have *this* to share. No one had built a case for publishing the five pages against the will of the United States government, in particular the National Security Agency, from which the document had originated if indeed it was real. It was as if, one staffer told me, a note had been taped to a rock and thrown over a wall. In the analog era you might meet your source in a parking garage, and in the digital era you might launch an encrypted conversation on your phone, but this source had done neither. Truly anonymous leaks were, even here, anomalous. And there was the economy of it; not the hundreds of thousands of digital files leaked by Manning and then by Snowden, but five pieces of paper relating to one issue at the center of one conflict being waged on cable news. There was no sea of documents through which to wade.

The P.O. box in which it was found was rarely used and rarely checked. When it was checked, the box was usually, according to one staffer, full of "time-wasters" addressed to a couple of *The Intercept*'s most glamorous personalities. When, in May 2017, a young reporter took the key to the box around the corner, he found a standard white envelope postmarked AUGUSTA. It had been sitting there, it seems, for at least a couple of weeks.

The young reporter who didn't usually check the P.O. box because it was full of time-wasters opened the envelope. The document was labeled TOP SECRET and marked SI, or special intelligence, which is to say it was derived from intercepted communications. It was marked ORCON, which stands for "dissemination and extraction of information controlled by originator," though in this case that had not been true.

"This report," states a boxed message on the first page, "includes sensitive technical information related to computer network operations that could be used against US government information systems."

The young reporter gave it to someone who worked on what he called, in internal interviews after the fact, "Russia stuff." The staffer who worked on Russia stuff showed it to another staffer and asked if she thought it was real. She thought it might be.

A German reporter once suggested to me that the single document reflected a kind of thoughtfulness on the part of the leaker. "The leaker," she said, "had made it so easy for them."

It would of course not go easily for them; it would go so disastrously that it would end an era of publishing internal documents from government sources known or unknown. I have come to see this not as a failure of journalism, though it was also that, but as a failure of imagination. It was hard to look at the five pages full of acronyms—"SI//ORCON/REL," it said across the top—and conjure a person. It was hard to imagine that person tearing off a sweat-soaked shirt after a CrossFit workout, feeding a twitchy dog, insisting a sister watch *Orange Is the New Black*. A person you cannot imagine is a person whose safety you will treat with a certain lightness.

It wouldn't have been enough, though, to conjure the sender, because the sender was embedded in a system borne of a world, and the five pages existed, in part, to create distance from that world.

Say it starts with Carlton Douglas Ridenhour, professionally known as Chuck D, vocalist of Public Enemy, moralizing purveyor of socially conscious hip-hop, given to sample-heavy lectures on the evils of cheap liquor, apathy, and corporatism. It was to this improving genre that fourteen-year-old John Lindh was drawn: Jeru, Grand Puba, Ice Cube, men who believed that something was deeply amiss in the structure of society. At eleven years old, John is a beautiful boy with big brown eyes. He asks his mother to take him to the film *Malcolm X,* and he loves the scene where Malcolm and hundreds of thousands of others venture to Mecca and kneel in unison. This is thrilling to him: racial unity through obedience. Here was an early taste for the experience of losing a sense of the edges of embodiment, the experience of ecstasy. It is an odd moment for an American boy to love, a physical display of collective submission in Saudi Arabia, but it takes an American sensibility to think: *That could be me.* John had chronic, socially isolating stomach problems that kept him out of school. His mother would later describe him as easily frightened.

Self-invention is the task that America presses on its white suburban adolescents. Outside John's bedroom lay newly paved roads and tree-covered hills, a stay-at-home mother, a playful, admiring younger sister, a father who worked late as lead counsel for an energy conglomerate. He was a brunet with the thick features of an awkward teen. This canvas was distressingly blank, but online, John could pop. Online he claimed to be Black, wrote his own rap music, and tended to push for what he saw as an authentic blackness against the corrupting influences of money, white people, and vice. "Our blackness does not make white people hate us; it is THEIR racism that causes the hate," he writes in a post calling out, from the comfort of his bedroom in Northern California, *another* poster for pretending to be Black. Through these early hypocrisies he was playing with ideas of purity; the music he loved had to be appreciated in its unadulterated form. People who believe the enjoyment of hip-hop requires drugs and alcohol are, in his words, "worthless dickriders."

In our century we are accustomed to stories that carry us from the physical to the digital. Once, there was a person in an office you could visit to make travel arrangements. That person smelled of wood chips, and the brown envelope of tickets he handed you was rough to the touch. It's not that the world is no longer physical now that you engage only with pulses of light via plastic and liquified crystal and polarized glass; liquified crystal is as wholly matter as the travel agent's tie. It's that our *sensual* world is radically diminished. What does a screen smell like? John Lindh's story is this, but inverted; absence to sensuality. He found Islam online and hurled himself into a dramatically incarnate future. It took him only three years to travel from his sterile California bedroom to a fetid, flooded fortress where he waded through water filled with corpses, and, dehydrated nearly to death, struggled with the temptation to drink.

A through line from Malcolm to Ice Cube and Public Enemy is the Nation of Islam. Lindh left his bedroom first for the Islamic Center of Mill Valley, a simple mosque housed in an old Baptist church, where a digital clock kept time on the minbar, and boys in sports jerseys touched their heads to the ground under a cheap chandelier. His parents, Buddhist and Catholic, were relieved that he had found a way out of his isolation, toward a community of gentle believers. It seemed healthy. That year he began wearing a robe in public. He grew an aspirational beard. A thing you can say about John Walker Lindh: He commits.

John told his mother that he wanted to learn Arabic, but not Arabic that had been tainted, not the Arabic of worthless dickriders—he wanted to learn it in the place where spoken Arabic most closely resembles that of the Koran. He and his mother researched schools in Yemen. There was one owned by a Yemeni married to a woman from Oregon. Marilyn called the school and spoke to the American owner. She decided to let her son follow his interests. He was a searcher. She helped him search.

In Yemen John was seventeen and out of his bedroom, cut off from screens. The streets were wide, the air thick with exhaust, the buildings all the color of sand. The school, full of rowdy Western expatriates, was terribly disappointing. Impure. No one around him sufficiently serious. The classes were coed, of which he disapproved. He complained to management. He complained to other students. "Dear Inhabitants of This Room," he wrote in a note he posted on another expat's door. "Please abstain from getting naked in front of the window." John learned that his mother and father would be separating. His father had been seeing another man.

After six weeks, John abandoned the school where people got naked in front of the window. He joined an immersion program at a Yemeni university, went home for ten months, and flew back east in the fall of 2000, eventually making his way to an obscure, spartan, independent madrassa in Pakistan, where he would be the only adult student among forty children. He kept in touch with his parents through letters and recited the Koran beside all the little boys. He was stripping life down to essentia, pursuing intimacy with a single text. The political organization he believed most faithful to that text was the Taliban.

Lindh scribbled over a picture of galloping horses on his notebook; he had begun to think visual art irreligious. In that notebook he had also begun cataloging atrocities against Kashmiri Muslims by Indian security forces: "60,000 Kashmiris have been killed, 26,000 wounded." "461 schoolchildren burned alive." "700 women raped." He had heard stories of tortured schoolchildren, in a conflict a day's drive away. How good it felt to feel the welling up of outrage, the singleness of purpose. *Four hundred sixty-one schoolchildren burned alive.* The stories you tell yourself on the way to the recruiting office. John Lindh is exactly my age, and this is the part of the story I return to again and again: a boy, twenty years old, hopping from home to madrassa, untracked, unclaimed. The absolute unwatchedness of his wanderings. Could any of us have done this? All the terrible ideas you had when you were twenty, the fanaticisms that come so easily, clean of consequence, ideologies unmarked by encounters with the world. What if you had acted on them? Historically, the United States government did not particularly care if young American men felt called to jihad. There were, in fact, Saudi-funded Muslim recruiting outfits in Brooklyn, Atlanta, Boston, Chicago, Pittsburgh, and Tucson, intended to connect American Muslims with Afghani mujahideen in Pakistan. Estimates of how many Americans joined up in the '80s range from dozens to many hundreds, but no one knows how many left because no one thought it sufficiently interesting to keep track. The thing on which you will one day focus all of your anxiety is not the thing you know, today, to fear.

Who are you? You are data about data. You are a web of social relationships. You are a map of connections. This morning in the car line at the Montessori school you called a pediatric dermatologist and spoke for two minutes, the time it takes to make an appointment. From Target, you called a ski instructor and spoke for seventy-two minutes, which is eight minutes longer than yesterday and twenty-three minutes longer than the day before that, which suggests an escalating interest in someone not your spouse. The ski instructor and you both receive emails from the Montessori school, which suggests that this is how you met. Both you and the dermatologist receive frequent texts from the Democratic Party. Both you and your spouse receive emails from the Audubon Society; you used to open these emails, but now only your spouse opens them. It is intuitive to think that it is the content of our communication that matters, the words of our emails, the turns of phrase with which we text. We want to believe we exist in what we choose to say, but this overstates our autonomy; we are at least as realized in our connections to other people. "A man," wrote sociologist Charles Cooley in 1901, "may be regarded as the point of intersection of an indefinite number of circles." To make themselves real, children invent imaginary friends.

It's too late, of course; you are already known, though the you that is known is not the you that you are. Willingly you have surrendered many bits of information that, taken together, form a sclerotic social identity with a strange relation to the real. Surveillance finds truths, and surveillance serves the creation of elaborate untruths. In our time we have cast disappearance as suspect—"ghosted," we say, as if it's a bad thing—while we celebrate the keeping of a kind of terrible track: *I have the receipts*. A paper receipt might get trashed or lost or misfiled, out of reach of digital discovery. But it is our fate to live in the age of the indelible. We all have to have the receipts, receipts for everything, receipts for texts and one-line emails and Facebook messages, an ageless record of the time I made a bad joke in a group thread and my friends twice-tapped *haha!* so as not to leave me hanging. To study surveillance is to learn, over and over, that we cannot escape ourselves.

It is the job of the National Security Agency to amass information from waves—calls and texts and internet searches. (The considerably less nerdy CIA collects information from bodies.) It is illegal for the NSA to target Americans (that's the FBI's job); it is the NSA's job to track foreigners. At the NSA they have long known that you can make precise predictions simply by knowing the location of people, who they are calling, and for how long. From this "metadata" one builds a picture, makes predictions; one concludes that the Montessori parent will not go on the birding trip with the spouse, but will abscond with the ski instructor. From this metadata, the intelligence community decides whom to kill.

In 2000 the National Security Agency was still getting used to the fact that the world had transformed nearly all of its communications into matter it could monitor. There were no more visits to the travel agent; everything was a signal, and thus the NSA's purview had expanded immeasurably. Its approach was to collect everything, which was not a good approach. The NSA had, in the past, intercepted suspicious communications by a Khalid, a Nawaf, and a Salem. There were many reasons information remained unexamined, and among those reasons was the scope of what had been collected. There was the problem, discussed previously, of too many selfies.

From the school full of children, thinking of jihad, John Lindh emailed his parents about weather: "In Bannu, it's starting to heat up," he wrote. And "Indian heat is not like Californian heat." He would go into the mountains, he said, in search of a better climate. He would later say he knew nothing of the Taliban's repression of half its population, nothing of the public practice of beating women with metal-studded sticks should they show their faces in public, and whether you believe this depends on how deep you allow for the thoughtless ignorance of a twenty-year-old driven by ideological passion, exposed to propaganda, and far from home. Certainly he was not a man who thought deeply about the subjective experience of women.

It's difficult to push yourself to the front lines of a foreign army that's never heard of you. Lindh found a training camp in Pakistan, where he hoped to be put to use in the defense of Kashmir. He was quiet and uncomplaining, but once again deeply judgmental; the place was too political, not sufficiently religious. "A fat farm of sorts for doughy Saudi teenagers," according to an ACLU report. He left after three weeks, looking for something more serious. In Afghanistan, Lindh found a Taliban recruiting office. It was June 2001.

Lindh was handsome now; slim, sun-drenched, his features had become delicate, cheekbones high and wide. He never would look like a fighter. It was not enough, to these recruiters, that John Walker Lindh desperately wanted to participate in the purifying of a Taliban-led Islamic State. It was not enough that he was now prepared to kill members of the Northern Alliance, the secular army battling for control of Afghanistan. To the recruiters, Lindh was not front-line material. He couldn't speak even one of the languages used by the regular Taliban forces—Urdu, Dari, Pashto. His training was laughable. The fat camp? Spend two weeks at a real training camp, they said, and you'll be allowed to join up not with the Taliban proper but a lesser force of Arabic speakers: Al Ansar, *the helpers*—Uzbeks, Arabs, Pakistanis. They were thought to be less predictable, more desperate and brutal.

The real training camp is the one you've heard of, days and nights in a canyon between barren, treeless mountains. Lindh was getting closer to the center of things, further and further inside the set of concentric circles around the ecstatic submission he sought. Al-Farooq was the place where Lindh would feel the weight of a rocket launcher on his spindly shoulders, and experience the oddly quiet, gentle kick of an AK-47. Here he grew accustomed to placing his hands around a grenade, round as a Christmas-tree bulb. He learned to navigate using the sun and the moon. He crawled through the canyon, sweating in the September heat, and stood up with his tunic covered in red dirt. He woke at 3:30 A.M. for washing, and then there were prayers and classes and speeches and meals until bed at 9:00.

The speeches were dull, Lindh said, and he fell asleep during one by a man who seemed slow and ill, surrounded by a flashy entourage Lindh thought ungodly. This was Osama bin Laden, of whom Lindh would later claim to know very little. The slow ill man was helping to fund the camp, which included both those training to be part of the Afghan army for a traditional war, as was Lindh, and, separately, those training for terrorist attacks on the United States, Israel, and elsewhere. Four future hijackers had trained here at some point. An instructor, toward the end, asked Lindh if he'd like to participate in jihad in Israel or the United States. Lindh said no, and was sent, as he wished, to Afghanistan, to fight in an obscure war with no obvious relationship to the U.S. His first day on the front line was September 6.

On September 11, 2001, Reality Winner—her real name, let's move past it now—was nine years old. That morning, she turned in a nine-page essay on her grandma Betty. She thought it was excellent, but her fourth-grade teacher at Ricardo Elementary pronounced it unreadable. The handwriting needed serious work. Reality was told to go home and rewrite the whole thing, from scratch, more carefully. Her mother took her to soccer after school, and Gary, her stepdad, coached. For reasons she didn't understand, no one actually practiced—the kids kicked a ball around while the grown-ups talked.

Reality went home in a rage. At the kitchen table, she tried to write each word in a way of which her teacher would approve, but it went so, so slowly. She wept in anger. Her mother gently encouraged her. Reality seethed. She wrote some more. The next day, the teacher rolled the television into the classroom. Reality and the other fourth graders watched two airplanes crash into the towers. They discussed different theories. They were eight and nine and ten years old.

Her first word had been *dada*. Her second, *no*. Reality's father was given to conspiratorial, nonconformist thinking; he was a smart man, you might say, with poor research skills. He would pass down to his youngest daughter an insistence on independent thought, though hers would be more constrained by fact. He instructed Reality to distinguish between Islam and Islamist extremists. He spoke of the importance of communication, the language and culture that separate us from the other. The day after the towers fell, Reality went to the Ricardo school library, took out the *A* encyclopedia, and found *Arabic*. She began tracing the first letter of the alphabet, *alif*, a single vertical line, with the intense focus of a child cracking a code. Reality had decided that she was going to stop the next attack. At home, she turned to the first page of *Fellowship of the Rings,* the map, and noted the way the illustrator had drawn mountains and topographic detail. She drew maps of Afghanistan, adding the same little shaded curves she had seen in the book. She folded her map, like something she'd take on a quest, something she'd carry with her to remember her purpose. This was the self-regarding melodrama of a preteen, but Reality was right to feel a sense of premonition. The course of her life had been set in motion.

John Lindh, twenty, did not know, as Reality did, that Afghanistan and the United States were newly entwined. He was cold and wind-chapped in the mountains of Takhar, dragging a rifle along a landscape that resembles nothing so much as the moon. He was a guard on a hill, bearded, hair down to his shoulders. He stared out onto bare valleys, never fired a weapon. He waited in shallow ditches dug into the side of the hill. They ate what the Taliban issued. The fighters were baffled by a bag of macaroni. "You can't just eat it," he said, taking the bag. "You have to submerge them in boiled water."

Lindh was told by other soldiers that Bin Laden had struck the United States. This seemed, from Lindh's perspective, to have very little to do with him. He did not work for Al Qaeda, the organization that had downed the towers. It did not seem to Lindh that the Americans had a quarrel with the Taliban. It seemed to him that they had a quarrel, quite unrelated to him, with Al Qaeda and Osama bin Laden. To leave his post defending the Taliban would have meant walking for two days in a lawless wilderness over frozen ground, but then, he never considered it.

Lindh is on the cusp of home, but home is a different place. His neighborhood is now covered in flags. There are flags on cars, front porches, ties. The president has a 90 percent approval rating. Congress had allocated $40 billion to fight terrorism; three weeks later, they'd added another $40 billion, and then there were many more spending bills:

In the words of one congressional chief of staff, "massive amounts no one could check." The president of Russia called the president of the United States to express his sympathy, offered help in tracking down the perpetrators, and agree to allow the United States to set up military bases in Central Asia; foreign policy analysts announced a new era of friendship between the two countries. The attorney general and others have written and passed, with almost no opposition, the Patriot Act, which made it easier for law enforcement to locate abstractions against which the country had united. The concisely and aptly named Authorization for Use of Military Force gives the president the power to do what he deems necessary, a law that would be used to justify thirty-seven military operations in fourteen countries, warrantless wiretapping, the drone programs, extraordinary rendition, Guantánamo. Most accounts of this time will refer first to fear, but fear is not what I remember feeling as an eighteen-year-old in the days after the towers fell. I remember, mostly, the thrill of clarity and common purpose. The temptations of certainty against a common enemy. I remember an angry, authorless speech played on a popular radio station, a deep voice exhorting us to *kick ass.* I remember my heart beating faster. The body thrilling to purpose.

Late 2001 was a time of leisure and plenty for military recruiters. "We face an enemy determined to bring death and suffering into our homes," the president said. The dreams of Americans showed an increase in "central image intensity." Where purpose had been muddy, it was now clean. The purpose of the state was to stop another attack. For years afterward servicemen and -women would give 9/11 as the reason for risking their lives, and whether this was catalyst or rationalization would remain mysterious perhaps even to them. Edward Snowden signed up in 2005, Chelsea Manning in 2009, Reality Winner in 2010.

In any story, there is a last moment in which the protagonist might have walked away, unbothered by consequence, but we are past that now. Had John Lindh left for his adventure a few months previous and come back home to enroll in a reasonably priced public university in California, it is entirely possible that no one would have known about his wanderings, and had anyone known, it's unclear anyone would have cared. He had traveled as far as he could from his bedroom, as if seeking the edge of the known universe, the place most decidedly private from the concerns of his family or neighbors. It is his enduring misfortune that in running from home he ran toward a conflict that became, immediately upon his arrival, the focus of American military power, surveillance, and fury.

YOU DON'T HAVE PERMISSION

Lindh walked for three days straight, with little food or water. Bombs tore off limbs, crushed heads, opened stomachs. Men waited outside the hospital for help, and pointed guns at emergency room doctors until they complied. The sky was full of planes. The Americans had arrived. They would be there for twenty years.

With the Americans supporting from the air, the Taliban were quickly overwhelmed. Lindh's unit was told they would be set free, sent home to the various countries from which they had come. He and 400 fellow fighters were taken by truck to a giant sandcastle, a mud fortress the same tawny shade as all the land around it. The walls of this fortress are thirty feet thick. It extends for a third of a mile and looks as if it were designed by an unimaginative child, flat and brown with craggy crenulations like uneven teeth. Lindh and the others were told to file into the seven-room basement of a small pink rectangular building within the fortress. They were not, in fact, being set free. They had been sold out by the Taliban.

John Lindh descended into the basement, dark except for a few tiny cutouts near the ceiling; men pressed up against one another to look outward. The prisoners had been told to leave their weapons in a pile, but they had not obeyed. In the darkness, they pulled guns from the smalls of their backs, from under bandages, shirt sleeves, pant legs. There are 400 of them now; 314 will die here.

John was brought up from the basement, to be interrogated. A soldier tied his elbows together and placed him on his knees in the courtyard, surrounded by many other tied-up Taliban. In a dusty expanse surrounded by sixty-foot walls, Lindh heard, for the first time in months, English. "Look at me," said a man in Western clothes, staring down at Lindh. "I know you speak English." His voice was surprisingly gentle. The accent American. Lindh thought he was a mercenary, but the man, Mike Spann, was CIA.

Lindh's body hunched, hair in his eyes. His feet were bare. The man knelt down, stuck a small camera in Lindh's face.

"What are you, puzzled? You know the people you're working with are terrorists? Push your hair back," the man said, but Lindh's elbows were tied. An Afghan soldier walked over and flopped Lindh's hair to the back of his head.

Lindh had done everything he could to escape his identity as an American, but it had followed him here. The fortress was quiet. Neither Spann nor Lindh could see the frenzy building within it, hundreds of angry armed hungry men who had been promised safe passage home and locked away.

When the gate opened to let out another group of men for interrogation, six prisoners forced their way out, shouting, throwing grenades. Prisoners in the courtyard stood up and ran; prisoners from the basement poured into the yard. Spann, in jeans, clearly a foreigner, was shot in the chest. He was thirty-two, his youngest child six months old, the first American military death after 9/11, the first death after the

American state united in singleness of purpose in the quest to stop a second attack.

Hungry prisoners fanned out and found trailers full of weapons: grenades, rifles. The Northern Alliance, never known for its competence as a fighting force, had essentially imprisoned its enemies, already armed, inside of an armory. Hours later, the yard was filled with dead men and horses. American planes dropped missiles that screeched through the air and threw up black plumes of dust. Ash fell on the cadavers of horses in the courtyard. Northern Alliance fighters with hard-worn shoes pulled better ones from the still feet of corpses. Now there were reporters everywhere: Americans and Germans and Brits with mics and tripod-mounted cameras. It was the center of the world.

Two days later the fortress was cleared, and the Northern Alliance had an interesting problem: a basement full of hostile men with guns. The Alliance fighters stood outside and thought of ways to murder the men inside. First the most obvious way: They aimed their guns at the tiny windows, and shot. They lobbed grenades through the holes. Shrapnel ricocheted off the wall and into John's shoulder, ankle, foot. John and the others tripped over corpses as they dodged the grenades. The air smelled like blood. Men climbed over other men to shit in the corner. John waited in the dark, inside, sick, and cold, and thirsty, listening to the *pit-pat* of bullets and screams of projectiles and, once in a long while, the blast of a missile.

This, not his religious intensity, is what so clearly separates John Walker Lindh from his time. As other people of his class and privilege moved away from sensory experience, increasingly connected not through touch but through wire, walled off by a proliferating number of screens, something in John Lindh sought animal suffering. As others let the auditory and olfactory, the ancient senses, become wholly subordinate to the visual, John, in the service of some evil about which he remained determinedly naive, allowed himself a holistic sensory onslaught. John hadn't eaten in days, and some of his toes were frostbitten. He would have done anything for a cup of water.

One day the Alliance fighters have a new idea. They pour fuel into the basement. John's tunic is soaked in gasoline. They light a match. Men burn alive. Lindh passes out to screams of other men, but he does not burn. On the sixth day, the Alliance fighters find a hose. They point it into the basement. The men are already losing toes to the cold. Now frigid water creeps up their feet, ankles, up to their knees. Limbs and excrement float to the surface. Men too wounded to stand simply drown. Lindh leans on a stick but falls, once, into the still water, under which are disembodied limbs, weapons, urine, shit. He pushes himself back up and stands, shaking from cold, for twenty hours. Lindh has not had a drop of water for days. When he is thirsty enough, he cups his hands, opens his mouth, and drinks.

At the CIA, hundreds of cubicles were organized in rows, and above those rows were signs: BIN LADEN BOULEVARD, WINSTON WILEY WAY—to help navigate the mess. "I'm the fourth cube on Bin Laden Boulevard," you might say. John Kiriakou, a Greek American CIA analyst, was still at Langley the day he learned about Lindh, though he was about to be sent to Pakistan to head counterterrorism operations in this new world. *If Mike's got to die,* he thought, *this guy's got to die too.* This feeling, we can assume, was widely shared.

The state's view of us, written with our cooperation, is a

sticky fiction. It assumes a permanent single self, for one thing, a lumbering anchored persistence. Hume called the self "a bundle of different perceptions, which succeed each other with an inconceivable rapidity, in perpetual flux." What connects us to our past selves? Not our cells, dead and replaced in the span of seven years, but unstable memories, colored by every conceivable cognitive bias. My memory is particularly bad, which is awkward at parties ("We have met *many times,*" the wife of a colleague recently told me at a faculty holiday event), but I ceased being sad about it when I realized the saddest people I knew had the most precise recall. They tend unwillingly toward trauma and grievance, too knowledgeable about the selves they last were, trapped in scenes of conflict they can too well reconstruct. Whereas I constantly stumble upon passages of this very manuscript I have no memory of writing, and think: *Delightful! I've escaped.*

Selves are mercifully fluid and multiple, and in the naive '90s this was the rapturous way people talked about the internet: a place where you could become anyone you wanted, create anything of which you could dream. I don't know that this is wrong. The internet is vision externalized. But whoever you become and whatever you make stays in the room with you. You have to live with it all forever, the bad takes tacked to the ceiling, scores of abandoned personae splayed over the bed, the teenage diction spilling out of the open closet door, crowded and uncomfortable, dense with unwanted memory. Typically we think of that which doesn't belong to us as literally out of reach, but the internet is a place where the thing you do not own may trail you for all time.

The end of anonymity comes in the form of a thick-bodied forty-six-year-old Canadian journalist and documentarian named Robert Pelton, author of the book *The World's Most Dangerous Places* and other works with "dangerous" in the title. Pelton had been hanging around the edges of battle, filming, pushing himself closer and closer into the action. He had heard about an American in the crowd. A doctor brought him into a room full of wounded on stretchers, and there is the boy, bearded, face smeared with mud, dried blood in his matted hair, lying on a stretcher. His eyes, half open, would not focus.

"What's your name?" asked a doctor, and rapped Lindh on the head.

"I'm John."

His accent was thick and his grammar odd, as though English were strange to him.

"Can I ask how you ended up here?" Pelton asked Lindh.

"Who are you who are filming?"

"I'm from the CNN news organization."

"All right. Look, you don't have my permission to film me."

"Okay that's not our concern right now," said Pelton, unconcerned enough to keep the camera on. "Our concern is your welfare."

"All right," said Lindh. "If you're concerned about my welfare then don't film me. And don't take pictures of me."

"How old are you?"

"Twenty years old."

"Twenty years?"

"Yes."

"Can I ask how you ended up here?"

"It's kind of a long story," he said, and laughed a little laugh.

Sometimes as he spoke he wrinkled his nose in pain, revealing straight white teeth. He was filthy with a bullet in his leg, but he was a twenty-year-old man, and the overall impression was one of persistent American health.

"Was this what you thought it would be?" Pelton asked.

"It is exactly what I thought it would be."

"And did you enjoy the jihad? I mean, was it a good cause for you?"

"Definitely."

Who are you? You are a web of social relationships. You are data about data. It's true that you called the ski instructor from Target and spoke for seventy-two minutes, which is eight minutes longer than yesterday and twenty-three minutes longer than the day before that, which suggests an escalating interest in someone other than your spouse. It is true that you were supposed to go on a birding trip with your spouse, who still opens the emails to the Audubon Society even though you don't open yours, and that you canceled and let the plane tickets go unused. But it's also true, to people who know you, that the ski instructor is your best friend, and has recently slipped back into an old addiction. It is also true, to people who know you, that the trip was canceled because your child has begun having troubles at school. You are a web of social relationships. Many, many stories can be spun from that web. "We kill people based on metadata," a CIA director once said, which is true, and they are often the wrong people.

On December 2, eighty-two days after 9/11, the footage was broadcast on CNN. John Lindh would be allowed only one identity in the end, but the contours of that identity were still being negotiated on cable news.

"Obviously, he has been misled," President Bush told the media shortly afterward. "It appears to me that he thought he was going to fight for a great cause. . . . We're just trying to learn the facts about this poor fellow."

"'Poor Fellow' or Traitor?" asked a headline in the *New York Post,* which went on to answer its own question, also in the headline. "Looks Like a Rat, Talks Like a Rat, Smells Like a Rat, Hides Like a Rat—It Is a Rat." Rudolph Giuliani, the mayor of New York City, admitted he didn't have "all the facts" but added, "I believe the death penalty is the appropriate remedy to consider." Hillary Clinton called him a "traitor." Diane Sawyer asked the president's parents what they thought of their son calling John Walker Lindh a "poor fellow."

"Well," said the president's mother, "I think the president meant that he's obviously demented."

"Sad," said the president's father.

"Sad," said the president's mother. "I think that's what the president meant. It is sad when someone is so sick, that he would cooperate with—"

"The enemy."

"That's right. The enemy. That's— That's right."

There was confusion about who, exactly, was the enemy. From a distance, it was hard for the casual American consumer of news to distinguish between Al Qaeda, an international organization that had tried to kill them, and the Taliban, an Afghan organization primarily interested in killing Afghans, and with which John Lindh had been found.

Even when distinctions were made, there was confusion. "Sources say Walker proudly informed his interrogators he was not merely Taliban but al Qaeda," *Newsweek* reported, but it turned out that the interrogator simply did not know the difference and wrote *al Qaeda* when Lindh said *al Ansar*. "Spann's Widow Says Taliban Kid Should Die," read an illustrative headline.

Is it possible that John Lindh had not thought the Taliban to be a haven for enemies of the United States, had not an inkling of what Osama bin Laden was plotting? I only know that when he and I were both eighteen, I was a student in Washington, D.C., and for some time, it was unclear which presidential candidate had won the election. Back home for Thanksgiving, an uncle asked me what it was like "to experience this in the capital." He expected me to have some particular insight. The only way I could think to answer was that there was no subway in Georgetown, so I couldn't know what was happening in Foggy Bottom, which is where I thought, incorrectly, that the White House was. In fact I lived in Washington, D.C., for seven years and never visited the White House. Had I visited the White House, this would not have led to any relevant insight about current events. I came by my knowledge the same way everyone else did. At a certain level of distance, proximity means nothing at all.

There is footage of Lindh after the battle, filthy on a truck in between two men. He is holding an orange in one hand and an apple in the other. "If you take pictures," he says, "don't use them without permission."

Lindh was handed over to American military personnel, confined to a dark room, and interrogated for days. He asked for a lawyer and was told none were available. Americans cut off his clothes, duct-taped his body to a stretcher, and told him to shut the fuck up when, weeping, he asked that the ties be loosened. When he had to pee they tilted the stretcher up. He shivered with cold in the Afghan winter. They left him this way for two days, and they took pictures. There were also the trophy shots: Lindh in a blindfold that read SHIT HEAD surrounded by smirking soldiers. "Don't take pictures without permission," he had said on the truck, always a few steps behind. His privacy had once been extraordinary in its scope.

Marilyn Walker found out about her son on MSNBC. By now Americans knew him as "the American Taliban." They would see him blindfolded, naked, duct-taped to a board.

Most of the men who lead at this time are secular men made sentimental by religious feelings, but the attorney general is a religious man made hard by patriotic feelings. Every day at 8:00 A.M., he held a public prayer meeting in a Department of Justice building to which any DOJ employee was welcome. He handed out stacks of devotionals, selected a passage, and read it repeatedly, until the group had committed it to memory. He believed in a reality shaped by biblical prophecy, but he had not been emotionally engaged by the idea of a terrorist attack.

As of September 11, the job was to prosecute terrorists. The attorney general didn't have any terrorists. He had a fellow religious believer, a man of another book, rigid and puritanical and given to rote memorization of a single sacred text. To someone not really interested in the details, John Walker Lindh was a perfect encapsulation of the problem. Flanked by flags, before a few dozen reporters, John Ashcroft put the United States back at the center of the story. The distinction between the Taliban and Al Qaeda disappears.

There was, according to the state, "a timeline of terror." Lindh was an "Al Qaeda–trained terrorist who conspired with the Taliban to kill his fellow citizens." He had trained with Al Qaeda, had "met with Bin Laden," and, after September 11, had elected to stay at his post, "shoulder to shoulder" with America's enemies. One cannot help but think of ecclesiastical authorities, against Galileo's protests, insisting on the centrality of home. The calculation is easy: *You're either with us or against us.* The key theme here is "us." If the United States could not be the hero of your story, it would frame itself as the great Satan. *I wasn't even thinking about you* is the excluded middle ground.

From within the Department of Justice, a young lawyer tells her colleagues that Lindh should not be interrogated without his lawyer present. He is interrogated anyway, against her advice. Once, the young woman who didn't think he should be interrogated without a lawyer had been on an episode of *The Phil Donahue Show*. The occasion had been an emergent situation with a bathroom wall at Brown University, where she was then a student. On the wall of the restroom of Rockefeller Library, women had written out the names of men they were accusing of assault. When the school found out, administrators set up a grievance procedure for the named men and ordered all graffiti scrubbed off. The names reappeared in Alumnae Hall. They were painted over. Beside Donahue was a giant cardboard version of a bathroom wall; as Donahue put it, "our re-creation of what you might find on the wall of the women's rooms at Brown University." Written on the cardboard: "____ ______ is a rapist. Nothing can get him off campus. Rich white boys can do whatever they want." In Donahue's re-creation, all the *i*'s were dotted with bubbly circles. Jesselyn Radack appeared onscreen, with three other activist students, in an oversized sweaterdress and dangly earrings. "If people think writing on the wall is ludicrous," Radack said, "I think it's ludicrous that when a man pleads guilty to rape the only punishment for him is that he has to write the victim—or I prefer to say *'survivor'*—an apology note." The chyron imposed over her read: ADVOCATE FOR LISTING NAMES OF RAPISTS ON BATHROOM WALLS.

After Lindh was interrogated, Radack suggested that the interview would not be admissible at trial, though it was admitted and in fact the prosecution's case hinged upon it. Later, when she was asked for a record of that email exchange to turn over to the judge, she could not find it. It looked to have been purged by an embarrassed DOJ. She recovered the emails with the help of tech support, printed them out, left them on her boss's chair, and walked out the door. Later Jesselyn would tell me that there is no personality shared by people who inform on organizations participating in illicit activity, but by then I had spoken to many such people, and I could see that there was such a personality, and she had it.

Jesselyn Radack has curly blond hair many women, or at least elite lawyers, would straighten, and the hair lends her an air of quizzical, sharp-edged judgment. She speaks with unusual fluency, as if the words were written out for her. While at Brown, she was diagnosed with multiple sclerosis. Her immune system was attacking her brainstem. She fought through fatigue to keep studying through Yale Law School, where one-third of her classmates applied to an honors program at the Department of Justice. She was one of two Yale students who got in.

The illness convinced her that she needed to accelerate

her plans. She would take no time off. She would get married and have her children early, while she was still strong. By 2000, before she had ever heard the name John Lindh, she was a thirty-year-old DOJ lawyer with two children, contemplating a third.

This was a time when many at CIA headquarters volunteered to go overseas, including John Kiriakou—the guy who wanted Lindh dead. He told anyone who would listen that he spoke Arabic, having picked it up for an old assignment in Bahrain. Four months after the 9/11 attacks, Kiriakou landed in Faisalabad, Pakistan, head of counterterrorism operations there. He was a thirty-seven-year-old analyst, and he was extremely well traveled and yet somehow not very cosmopolitan in the way of most people who travel exclusively to do the business of Americans. "Coke Light is what they call Diet Coke over there," he explains in his memoir, in which he also describes getting lost in Faisalabad and having to beg someone who worked at a McDonald's to draw him a map to another McDonald's on the back of a kids' menu because it was only from the second McDonald's that he knew the way home. He felt great. The work was exciting and truly at the center of something. Back home, he had left a bad first marriage and started something new and thrilling with a fellow CIA analyst named Heather.

At the time, Kiriakou had the politics with which he had gone to college: He was a hawkish liberal. At George Washington he had been part of the College Democrats, and when the other students issued a statement opposing the invasion of Grenada, he argued with them. It had seemed, at the time, very important what a half dozen college freshmen decided about the invasion of Grenada. Kiriakou has warm olive skin, thick black hair, and large, expressive eyes that tend toward vulnerability. He speaks with a crisp lucidity, zeroing in on the absurdity of any particular situation, but he also listens with unusual activeness. "Oh yes," he says repeatedly in conversation, "that is exactly right." According to both himself and a court-appointed psychologist, he is a devoted father. He is warm, emotive, present. There's a gentleness too, an almost feminine softness in his voice when he expresses regret for all that has transpired. One feels in his conversational generosity a kind of solicitous desire to be liked, and also a fascination with his own story. He rarely hedges or demurs; it is natural for him to express total commitment to any idea he holds, even if the idea is that his total commitment to an idea he recently held was ill-informed.

In 2002 Kiriakou and others were supposed to take down Abu Zubaydah, said to be Al Qaeda's number three. They could narrow his possible locations to twelve, so the Pakistanis with whom they were working would need to conduct twelve simultaneous raids. It was relatively easy for Kiriakou to blend in by growing a thick beard and wearing *shalwar kameez*. "Okay guys," he claims to have said as he stepped onto a coffee table in Pakistan, "I don't mean to be melodramatic, but we are going to have to synchronize our watches." At the makeshift CIA headquarters, there was a board with Zubaydah's phone number at the center, and around it many more phone numbers discovered by NSA and Pakistani surveillance. Here were the people who made him who he was. A contact chain.

The CIA paid the Pakistanis $10 million to make it happen. In a building in Faisalabad, Pakistani forces shot Abu Zubaydah in the stomach, testicle, and thigh. He was a man already damaged, by his time as a mujahideen, fighting against the Soviets and cheered on by the Reagan administration. He had a head injury that left him with a terrible memory. The only way he could remember anything was to write it down, so he kept thick diaries full of drawings and spare thoughts. When the CIA came through his safe house they'd find 10,000 pages of notes written to his future self, whom he calls Hani—the name his mother used for him.

"Dear thirty years old Hani," he writes in an early note, dated 1990, when he was nineteen. "Today, I have decided to write my memoirs and these words are to you. So, this will be the letter in which I complain to you, get things off my chest, and cry in your arms whenever I feel the need to share my burden, from this silly world, with someone."

FBI investigators would later argue that this familiar device of writing to the self was evidence of a "schizophrenic personality." The notes would not be returned to their author. Zubaydah would have to start new ones in his new life lived within America's new network of secret prisons. He would later tell his American lawyer that he could not remember his mother's face.

Zubaydah was taken to a hospital where the windows were open, mosquitoes floated in at will, and geckos darted about the ground feasting on the mosquitoes. Kiriakou, tasked with standing over the prisoner, says he watched a nurse sterilize a needle by running it under tap water and plunging it into a bar of Irish Spring. Kiriakou ripped up a sheet and tied Zubaydah to the bed. He ate meals out of hospital vending machines. He hadn't been able to change for days, so he asked someone to bring him fresh clothes from where he was staying. This is how he came to be wearing a bright red SpongeBob SquarePants T-shirt when Abu Zubaydah woke up. Kiriakou asked him, in Arabic, what his name was. In English, Zubaydah asked Kiriakou to kill him.

One can argue, with hindsight, that it would have been better if Kiriakou had done so, in that what lay ahead was a kind of darkness so profound that the agency would destroy the evidence and request that Zubaydah stay isolated forever such that he could never share the horrors to which he had been subjected. But Kiriakou did not kill Zubaydah. That was the last the two saw of one another, and the beginning of the end of Kiriakou's life as a spy in good standing.

Before Lindh ever got to the fortress, perhaps before he even knew of the attack, official American policy was changing in ways hard for the public to see, in part because many of the policies that were changing were those that made it possible for the public to know when policies were changed. The president approved death-by-drone. Every congressperson but one, Barbara Lee, signed a single joint resolution that would be used to justify surveillance of Americans, torture of suspects at secret prisons, the investigation of Americans by their own intelligence agencies. The vice president began traveling with a duffel bag, in which was a chemical-biological suit.

Much of the trait we call "agreeability" involves an ability to let things go, even when doing so presents a moral conflict. Within a month Jesselyn had a new job in private practice, a short walk from the DOJ, with a private firm. When they asked her why she left the ethics department, she said that she had left because the department was unethical. On the drive to work, she worried over whether the extra emails she had printed and dramatically left on her boss's chair had ever made it to the judge. John Lindh was in a prison cell, perhaps for the rest of his life, and the prosecution was leaning heavily on statements he had made in the interview Jesselyn had told them, in the purged emails, should not be allowed. While getting dressed for work, she heard an NPR report in which the DOJ claimed it had *never* asserted that Lindh was entitled to a lawyer, which Jesselyn knew to be false. She took this to mean that the judge had never gotten the emails, though there was no way to know, because the court filings were classified.

The next morning she heard Michael Isikoff, the *Newsweek* reporter who had broken the Monica Lewinsky story, on the radio, giving the DOJ's version of events. She looked up Isikoff and sent him the missing emails.

The cover of *Newsweek* on June 24, 2002, read "Fixing Your Brain" over an image of a dead-eyed woman's face. Along the seam: "Bionic Eyes and Ears." Inside was Isikoff's article: "The Lindh Case Emails."

The DOJ Office of the Inspector General, charged with investigating "waste, fraud, and abuse," called days later. An agent left multiple messages on her voicemail. His questions were about her schedule, her contacts. He told both a receptionist and a partner at her law firm that she was under criminal investigation, at which point she was asked to resign from her new job. Soon after that, she was informed by the inspector general that she had been referred for criminal investigation, a fact that she would have to divulge in job interviews, which made it impossible to find a new job after losing the last one.

The case against John Lindh was not going well. The attorney general had announced ten charges that would have carried more than three life sentences in prison. The defense argued that the confession on which most of those was based had been extracted via torture. A hearing was scheduled in which John Lindh would testify about the conditions under which he was kept—strapped to the board, freezing, hungry, confined to a shipping container—and in which the lawyer issue would come up. The government did not want John Lindh to testify about the way he had been treated or the way his confession had been extracted. They agreed to drop almost all of the charges, leaving only a charge of "supplying services" to the Taliban and a criminal charge for packing a rifle and two grenades while doing so. Those charges did not add up to three lifetimes, but they added up to a quarter of one: twenty years in prison.

"Had I realized then what I know now about the Taliban I would never have joined them," he told the court at his sentencing hearing. He was crying.

"Life is making choices and living with the consequences," the judge said. "You made a bad choice to join the Taliban."

It was in Isikoff's article in the magazine with the dead-eyed woman on the cover that Jesselyn learned, with everyone else, the emails actually had been given to the judge. The judge had simply deemed them unnecessary to share with the defense. There had been some sort of filing error. Her leak had been based on a misperception. There had been no conspiracy. The rules had not been broken. The problem went deeper than that; it was in the structure itself. The problem was in the rules.

ZERO
HIPPO

Dari and Pashto were two of the languages John Lindh could not speak and without which he could not join the Taliban's general forces. They were both languages Reality Winner was taught by the American military, along with Farsi, a decade after Lindh was sent to prison. The job was to stop another attack, and in the service of this goal Reality Winner was meant to sit in a cubicle in Maryland and eavesdrop on Pakistani men day after day and never tell anyone outside the building what she had learned.

The existence of a drone program was a secret. The legal justification for the drone program was a secret. It was a secret that through a program called SOMALGET the National Security Agency was recording and archiving the content of every single cell phone conversation in Afghanistan, and it remains unknown what percentage of conversations in Pakistan. It was a secret that algorithms then combed through these conversations and routed concerning ones to linguists like Reality Winner, who gisted—paraphrased—anything that seemed important. It was not much of a secret, however, to the men on whom she eavesdropped. They knew America was listening, just as they knew that the high-pitched drones above them transmitted video data back to the States, a long-running film of their daily lives. In western Pakistan, men got high on khat over lunch and told dirty jokes while she listened.

My friend's toddler calls shadows "zero" things; the shadow of a hippo is a "zero hippo," the shadow of herself "zero me." A zero America precedes even the name, but after 2001 government in secret was unfathomably well funded. Much of it remains literally hidden: in bunkers underground, or in the vast underground netherworld of dystopian Crystal City. But much is hidden by virtue of its ability to blend into corporate landscape too dull to take in: glassy buildings you float past without processing their existence, mile-long office parks behind straight lines of spindly trees. They have names such as *National Business Park* and *L-3 Communications,* names that in their intentional forgettability oppose the purpose of naming; often there is no exterior signage of any kind. Sometimes they are siloed in clusters of bland buildings, but the secret state also dispersed itself amidst extant office buildings. There are floors of D.C. buildings not listed in the lobby's directory. Government agencies few Americans had heard of spent amounts of money few could fathom; the National Geospatial Agency built itself a $1.8 billion facility in the bland suburb of Springfield, Virginia, that, in the literalism prevalent in so much public art and architecture, looked from above—or from a drone—like a giant eye. The head of the army's intelligence school described all this new construction as being "on the order of the pyramids," but the pyramids are spread over a much smaller geographic area. The "alternative architecture" of secret America, as journalist Dana Priest calls it, extends from D.C. to Tampa to Indianapolis to Salt

Lake to San Antonio and beyond, in landscapes so dull as to seem staged: office parks with ghostly Starbucks and unused gyms flanked by extended-stay hotels. Each secret program established by the government was serviced by an army of contractors hawking technical skills, language skills, data entry, each CEO well aware that a seemingly limitless amount of money was available and oversight nonexistent.

The currency of zero America is the secret, but the currency is degraded. Documents are marked classified for no particular reason, because it's always safest, because they may be potentially embarrassing, because no one takes a document not marked secret seriously. FOIA requests have unearthed a fan letter from J. Edgar Hoover to his favorite baseball player, the state of Florida's list of rejected license plates (DRUNK), an agreement between the 2012 movie *Battleship* and the U.S. Navy in which the navy is promised ten DVDs of the movie, the FBI's dictionary of Twitter slang ("L8R G8R" for *later, gator*). Thousands of new programs absorbed billions of dollars, generating new, mostly banal secrets, plenty of them public information easily gleaned from Google.

Upon his return to Langley, Kiriakou wrote a paper about Iraqi nuclear weapons and sent it to the Department of Energy, which has its own classification system. As he pressed SEND, it became illegal for him to access the paper he had written; he did not have the clearance. Kiriakou wanted to tell the president, as the military was preparing to invade Iraq, that someone had had a nervous breakdown. "I knew he had had a nervous breakdown," he told me at his kitchen table in Clarendon, "because I saw the original data, but I couldn't tell anybody that he had a nervous breakdown, because it was so highly classified, so highly compartmentalized. I couldn't put it in writing, because before it gets to the president, it goes through six other people, who wouldn't be cleared for the information." The president never found out; the information hit a dead end with Kiriakou. Kiriakou wanted to tell the president that a report had come in showing that a high-placed Iraqi source was unreliable and unstable. He knew the director of the CIA was about to meet with the president. But he couldn't print out the information—it was too highly classified, there was no PRINT option—or tell the director of the CIA's assistant, who was not cleared, so he remembered the report as best he could, ran up to the director's office, and told him. "Give me the report," the director said. "I'm not going to remember that stuff." Kiriakou said he couldn't print it out. He repeated what he knew, from his memory, three times. The director then repeated what he could remember to the president. Anyone who has played telephone can see the problem, though in this case the original information was later revealed to be false. It's hard to get people to fact-check information when no one can see it.

"I could count on my two hands the times that I used my open telephone in those fifteen years," he told me, "because everything is classified, including the classified email system. So I want to meet my wife for lunch, so I send her an email. 'You wanna meet for lunch?' And I classify in secret note form. Why? Because everything is classified. Everything. Like I would have to stop and think, should I really make this unclassified? So eh, fuck it, I'm just gonna say secret note form. That's what everybody does, for everything."

The secret state reveals itself in its need for people with security clearance to sift through emails about inviting one's wife to lunch. On clearedconnections.com, employers based in forty-seven states try to rustle up cleared candidates; at the time of writing, just one company, Northrop Grumman, to which Kiriakou would one day send half-naked pictures of his wife, had 2,250 job postings. In 2003, two million people had security clearance, approaching 1 percent of the population, which suggests less a security state than a caste system. Checking the backgrounds of so many Americans costs billions more. A zero state that keeps metastasizing would eventually become a world in which the majority are holding secrets from the few remaining people ineligible.

One petabyte of information is equivalent to twenty million four-drawer filing cabinets filled with text. At one intelligence agency, one petabyte of classified data accumulates every year and a half. Sifting through a petabyte of information in a year would require two million employees; around 100,000 people work in intelligence for the government. "There are billions and billions of documents, and there are like sixteen people declassifying everything," says Kiriakou. "So the email about meeting my wife for lunch will never be declassified, never."

On a base in New York in 2009, the army gave a twenty-one-year-old soldier raw war footage from which she was supposed to write reports for the higher-ups. All day long Chelsea Manning watched acts of war take place on a screen and tried to process them. She had access to all sorts of footage taken from above, alongside the recorded voices of soldiers watching it, all in Iraq, where the mission to stop another attack had metastasized. There was a grainy black-and-white video of a Baghdad suburb, seen from a helicopter above, palm trees and low square buildings and hauntingly empty sidewalks. That day in the suburb, men had been shooting at American soldiers. When the men in the helicopter saw Iraqis with various black objects slung over their shoulders gather on a street corner, they got very excited. The Iraqi men walk casually into the frame. Two of them—though the American soldiers do not know this—are journalists stringing for Reuters. One is Saeed Chmagh, a forty-year-old driver and camera assistant with a wife and four children at home. The other, a twenty-two-year-old celebrated photographer named Namir Noor-Eldeen. There are men in the group carrying actual weapons. The journalists carry only cameras. Manning saw what the American soldiers saw from above and listened to them negotiate the lives of the Iraqis below.

"That's a weapon," says an American voice. "Fuckin' prick."

"Request permission to engage."

"You are free to engage," comes the response.

"All right, we'll be engaging."

"Just fuckin' once you get on 'em, open up!"

They engage. The helicopter shoots eight-inch-long exploding tubes, ten of them in a second. They weigh—each individual round—a half pound. From the helicopter they whir: *duh-duh-duh-duh-duh-duh*. The visual disappears behind a cloud of dust and smoke, then resolves into a pile of bodies.

"Keep shooting, keep shooting!"

Mostly, they are still; it seems like less of a firefight than a light switch. Men on, then off. Except, that is, for Saeed, the driver, who, as the smoke resolves, is running along the side of the building.

"I got 'em!"

The Americans laugh.

"I hit him."

Saeed squirms on the ground. His legs are splayed. He's shaking. He is, one suspects, thinking of his children. There are four of his own, but he supports three more, and also the children of his sister, since her husband was killed. He talked about his kids all the time on long drives with journalists.

"Got a bunch of bodies laying there."

"Yeah we got one guy crawling around down there."

"Oh yeah look at those dead bastards."

"Nice."

"Good shootin'."

"Thank you."

"Come on, buddy," says a soldier, as if to Saeed, "all you gotta do is pick up a weapon."

Saeed never had a weapon. But should he pick up what looked like a weapon—the camera—the Americans would have permission to shoot him again.

"We have a van approaching and picking up bodies," says an American.

A van swerves into the scene. A man jumps out to help Saeed and carry his limp body into the van. What the Americans do not see, but is visible should you look for it, are two small heads peeking out the front window on the passenger's side. A little girl and a little boy watch.

"Can I shoot?" asks an American. He's talking about the van.

"Come on, let's shoot!"

Duh-duh-duh-duh-duh.

A smashed mirror flips off the van and falls to the ground. When the van comes into focus again, there's a massive hole in the windshield.

Now it is time for ground troops. A soldier runs from the

van with a little girl in his arms. She is four, and she is bleeding. There is windshield glass lodged in her eyes. The boy, eight, has shrapnel in his brain.

After silence, the voice, again, of the Americans in the helicopter.

"Well it's their fault," one says, "for bringing their kids into a battle."

The view of Iraq from the sky became so familiar to the soldier that when she was transferred to a base near Baghdad, the layout was known to her. Now it was simply real; one could feel the wind that moved the trees onscreen. One could hear the car bombs. But it was just a closer screen. Real and not real. The world she watched all day and the one she emerged into, safe. There's nothing remarkable, after all, about two tiny children irreparably damaged in a war zone. What is new is that she can call up the footage. The soldiers were under surveillance as they killed a man who held not a gun but a camera.

Her workplace was called a SCIF, a sensitive compartmented information facility, but was really a bunch of plywood thrown up on top of a basketball court. She sat at the free throw line, and in all the accounts I have ever read of Chelsea Manning spilling America's most shameful secrets, I have never seen it noted that it was here where it would occur to her to blow the whistle. Security was such that analysts kept passwords on sticky notes stuck to their laptops. Days on the job were long and boring and left plenty of time to dig deep, scanning the system for anything of interest, in a way not dissimilar to other twenty-two-year-olds digging into the internet that happened to be available to them. "I don't believe in good guys versus bad guys any more," she said, via chat, to the hacker who would eventually betray her. “Only see a plethora of states acting in self-interest, with varying ethics and moral standards, of course, but self-interest nevertheless. I mean we’re better in some respects, we’re much more subtle, use a lot more words and legal techniques to legitimize everything. It’s better than disappearing in the middle of the night, but just because something is more subtle, doesn’t make it right. I guess I’m too idealistic.” She is a person emerging from adolescence, negotiating ethical questions, as self-serious as any undergraduate taking a first course in philosophy, realizing that her parents had been wrong about everything, eager to set them straight and convinced that a straight-setting is possible. I am not mocking this moral seriousness and ambition. I miss it.

On leave in D.C. for a bit, she bought women’s clothes and rode the metro with no purpose but to be female in a public space. On the laptop brought from Iraq was classified data illegally downloaded. In the United States she was surprised to discover how few people were discussing the bloodshed she’d spent all day watching. “There were two worlds,” she later said. “The world in America, and the world I was seeing. I wanted people to see what I was seeing.”

Zero America was conceived in a time when the legitimacy of the state was assured, unquestioned. But the state’s infrastructure was hard and solid and the sense of legitimacy a mist already burning off. The structure would outlast the faith that built it. Julian Assange established WikiLeaks in 2007. It was a list of links. It was “an uncensorable Wikipedia for untraceable mass document leaking.” “We’re going to crack the world open,” Assange said. He cited Aleksandr Solzhenitsyn and compared himself to academics forced to labor in Russian camps. “True belief begins only with a jackboot at the door. True belief forms when led into the dock and referred to in the third person. True belief is when a distant voice booms 'the prisoner shall now rise' and no one else in the room stands." He released a report about the corrupt president of Kenya. A copy of the British counter-insurgency manual. A cache of emails from a speechwriter to Hugo Chávez. He couldn't get the mainstream media to cover the documents. If he had cracked the world open, no one cared to look down the chasm.

DIESEL REEZLE

Reality Winner grew up in a carefully kept manufactured home on the edge of a cattle farm a hundred miles north of the Mexican border in a majority-Latino town where her mother, Billie, still lives. From the back porch, a carpet of green meets the horizon, and when a neighbor shoots a gun for target practice, a half dozen local dogs run under the trailer to hide. Billie worked for Child Protective Services, and in Ricardo, Texas, the steady income made her daughters feel well-off; the fact that they had a dishwasher seemed evidence of elevated social standing. Billie, a chatty redhead with the high-pitched voice of a doll, supported the family while her husband, Ronald, she says, "collected degrees." It was Ronald who named Reality. The deal had been that Billie got to name their first—Brittany—but their second was his to choose. He noticed, on a T-shirt at their Lamaze class, the words I COACHED A REAL WINNER. He wanted a success story and felt that an aspirational name would increase his chances of producing one. Billie did not object; a deal is a deal.

Ronald was intellectually engaged, though never, during his marriage, employed, and Reality's parents separated in 1999, when she was eight. Her father was given to long, intense conversations about geopolitics, and happy to have them with his young daughters. He was careful to distinguish for them the religion of Islam from the ideologies that fueled terrorism, and from these first conversations Reality began to think about the relationship between language and peace. Her favorite subject in school was Latin, because in learning Latin she learned "the very structure of language itself."

Reality was a comically mature adolescent, intellectually adept, impatient with her peers, with a compulsive drive to improve herself she would eventually channel into an obsession with nutrition and exercise. Her body was strong and substantial and unadorned: thin blond hair tied up, light makeup, clothes that suggested a lack of interest in the act of dressing. She was shy and shyly mischievous. In the eighth grade, she organized a food fight so intense that she was banned from walking during graduation, though her mother points out that she was careful not to schedule it during spaghetti day, when it would have been especially messy.

Reality agreed to date her high-school boyfriend, Carlos, on certain conditions intended to improve and to edify. Carlos, who was failing out of school and broke, had to read a particular number of books a week. He had to maintain at least a C average. He had to get a job. He did not have clothes suitable for employment, but Reality would work on that; she had her mother take Carlos shopping for khakis and a polo. "Reality takes in a lot of strays," says her mother, "and I don't mean just animals."

She was a talented, stylish painter, and her most frequent subjects were herself, Nelson Mandela, and Jesus. She was an inveterate smasher of phones. She threw one across the room while talking to her father, who struggled with an addiction to painkillers and who she sensed was stoned, and cracked another one falling from a tree she'd climbed in a fit of whimsy. A third phone met its fate when it simply wasn't working. "How hard is it to be a phone?" she yelled, threw it, smashed it. She had a mean streak. She'd stop talking to you on a dime. She'd worry about the state of Syria, volunteer all of her free time, but she might not think to ask a friend how she was doing. There is a difference between being good and being nice.

Reality was raised six miles from a naval base, in a household where humanitarian and military motives were not taken to be in tension, at a moment when the country had mostly unambivalent feelings about the moral might of its armed forces. "What could be more humanitarian," Billie asks, "than protecting your country and innocent victims of war and terrorism?" As an adolescent, Billie had dreamed of joining the air force herself but ended up advocating for abused and neglected children as a social worker. During the summer before Reality's senior year, she called an army recruiting office and said, "Hi, I'd like to be a linguist for Middle Eastern and North African languages." The recruiter laughed, but when she drove to Corpus Christi, took the military's language aptitude test, and got twice the score of anyone else in the room, they offered to obtain a waiver so she could sign up immediately, and never have to be a senior at all. Reality told them she would be finishing school, despite the fact that one of the recruiters was "like a young Hispanic Arnold Schwarzenegger." Billie pushed the air force over the army. Air force recruiters begrudgingly agreed to meet Reality in the parking lot of a Whataburger;

they were skeptical of her, and she of them—"skinny pasty white dudes" she called them—but once again she overcame their doubts with test scores, and this time she connected with a woman recruiter who understood her ambitions. She would join the air force after graduation.

No one was surprised when Reality's sister, Brittany, went on to college, absurd amounts of college, such that she walked out of Michigan State with a PhD in pharmacology and toxicology and authored papers with titles such as "Metabolism of Dopamine in Nucleus Accumbens Astrocytes Is Preserved in Aged Mice Exposed to MPTP." But Reality had then, and has now, a skepticism of academic degrees, which she described to me as "hundred-thousand-dollar pieces of paper that say you've never had a job." ("It's interesting," her mother notes, "because of her father?") She wanted her life to start. There was a war going on, and she wanted to be part of it. She imagined herself overseas, translating under threat of fire, work given meaning by an air of danger. It wasn't until she was getting on the bus for basic training that she told her mother she'd applied to engineering school at Texas A&M–Kingsville, received a full scholarship, and turned it down.

At the NSA her life, according to those closest to her, involved an exceptionally punishing exercise regimen, volunteer work, and twelve-hour shifts listening to the private conversations of men and women thousands of miles away. There was also anxiety. Reality worried about global warming. She worried about Syrian children. She worried about famine and poverty all over the globe. Highly critical of her carbon-spewing, famine-ignoring fellow citizens, she nevertheless hoped her humanitarian impulses were compatible with the military's mission, and wished her fellow airmen were not just more competent in their jobs but more motivated to do them well, to save the vulnerable from acts of terror. She believed that change comes not just from within but from the top, which is to say that change involves patience. But patience would prove hard for her.

Reality was intellectual but she had not been raised in an intellectually sophisticated household. In this she resembles Edward Snowden and Chelsea Manning and Jesselyn Radack and Daniel Hale. An intellectual orphan comes to knowledge absent the social pressure to conform to a particular set of ideas. Reality would not have known which theories were fashionable or which to be slightly ironic about. It takes such a person, in their conceptual innocence, far longer to ably sort through the tangle of established human thought. But you cannot be subject to blind acceptance of received wisdom you have never received. She took ideas in their fullness, ignorant of their social context, and therefore radically open to argument. It did not matter to Reality that working for the drone program while teaching yoga and loudly moralizing about climate change would strike many people as bizarre. She was not on a team. Had not been invited to join one.

To those around her, Reality was a never-ending, frequently exhausting source of information on the world, its problems, and our collective obligation to pay attention. She gave her sister a marked-up copy of the Koran, rife with Post-it notes, and told her to read it. With an organization called Athletes Serving Athletes, she pushed wheelchair-bound kids through half-marathons. ("Athletes Serving Athletes," an ex-boyfriend told me. "She'd never shut up about that.") She donated money to the White Helmets, a group of volunteers performing search-and-rescue missions deep in rebel-held Syria. She told those around her to watch a documentary about racial injustice in the prison system, and another about abuses at SeaWorld.

On Facebook, where she called herself Reezle Winner because the site had rejected her legal name, she friended her yoga instructor, Keith Golden. *Who the fuck is Reezle?* Golden asked himself. Thereafter he called her "Diesel Reezle." He had, as everyone around Reality did, the sense that she was an extremely competent linguist. "I bet you dominate that military shit, they fucking love you, don't they?" he asked her.

"Well yeah," she said, "I'm good at my job."

What remained abstract and distant to the news-consuming public was neither abstract nor distant to Reality. She could spend an entire lunch with Golden despairing over atrocities committed by ISIS and her own inability to do anything about it.

The people closest to her did not know precisely what Airman Reality L. Winner did during her twelve-hour shifts at Fort Meade. They only knew that there were certain days when she knew something big was coming and went to bed early. Reality told her mother that she might have PTSD. If she were to explain the nature of her work stress to a therapist, she would risk being charged with espionage. If she were to admit to having PTSD, she would give up the opportunity to be deployed, which is to say she would be consigned to the cubicle for even longer. She exercised, and she journaled. She kept thick diaries full of small text, Post-it notes stuck to the margins. She wrote down instructions, inspirational quotes, arguments she was having with herself. A couple of times a week, for hours at a time, she would talk to her father, whose health was failing but who was constantly watching the news. They discussed the war in Syria.

Reality was tracking the kinds of places John Lindh had frequented, but she would not, as he had, get to wander. "It was definitely traumatizing," says an ex-boyfriend. "You're watching people die. You have U.S. troops on the ground getting shot at, you miss something, a bomb goes off, and you get three people killed."

She thought about Snowden and she thought about Manning and she thought about WikiLeaks. Sometimes she let herself read about all of it, but this always felt fraught; there was so much she, as a person with clearance, was not supposed to know. If she read an article about Snowden on her personal computer, and that article left a memory of itself somewhere deep in the machine, she could, she believed, be violating the law, though what law precisely remained hazy to her.

Reality was, her mother says, at war, though if we take this to be true it is a kind of war that offends a certain kind of warrior, the kind given to quoting the *Iliad* and worry about whether war itself has lost its ability to give meaning. The kind, in other words, to seek meaning from war. The intuitive argument against drones is that they introduce space between target and assassin; that they remove the element of danger from the act of killing. This is true, and disturbing, and also an argument that has followed every advance in military technology beyond, say, the perfect reciprocity of the swordfight: there was safety too behind a cannon. Guns were considered cowardly. Snipers were cowards, and men who fired from submarines.

Drones used to be purely eyes. You couldn't drop a missile from a drone without breaking the drone. It wasn't until February 2001, when Reality was nine, that the U.S. successfully shot a missile from a slim gray wasp into a green tank in Nevada. A week after 9/11, George Bush signed a memorandum authorizing targeted killings.

Would you rather be invisible or able to fly? Why not both? The most disturbing thing about drones, I once thought, was the transformation of combat into a video game, picking off military-aged men and flying away without sticking around to see the consequences. The profound alienation between some nineteen-year-old in a trailer in Nevada, pointing a joystick, and the eighteen-year-old Pashtun father he would wipe out. But this idea of alienation does not describe the experience of the drone pilot or the linguist working together to build a story about violent men. This is an experience of deep, half-imagined, crazy-making intimacy. Day after day the drone will send video feed of the same man leaving the same house and returning again. Reality will listen to him call his mother, his children, his lawyer, his best friend. She'll become familiar with the patterns of his day, his worries, his quirks; and what she cannot know, her imagination will build out. At night, when the infrared camera is operative, people appear as red blobs. It is hot, and they go on the roof to sleep. "I saw them having sex with their wives," said one drone pilot. "It's two infrared spots becoming one." A lit cigarette is a sun bobbing before a mouth. This is not the straight path of increasing distance between assassin and target. This is something new.

Reality participated in something that swept people from the lands she oversaw. A commendation she received in October 2016 praises her for "assisting in geolocating 120 enemy combatants during 734 airborne sorties." She is commended for "removing more than 100 enemies from the battlefield." She aided in "650 enemy captures and 600 enemies killed in action." People to whom she listened were killed, and when a drone kills someone, it lingers. Drone operators watch families retrieve limbs from exploded bodies.

There is intimacy and there is uncertainty. Cell phones are wave-spitting little beacons we carry with us, and these are what drones track, not people. "It's stunning the number of instances when selectors are misattributed to certain people," a young man named Daniel Hale told *The Intercept*'s Jeremy Scahill as "anonymous," before he leaked the documents known as the Drone Papers from his job at the National Geospatial Agency and before the FBI came for him. "And it isn't until months or years later that you realize that the entire time you thought you were going after this really hot target, you wind up realizing it was his mother's phone the whole time."

People switch cell phones, or lack them, and render themselves invisible. The visual you get from the drone, Hale explains, is so cloudy it's hard to make out a rifle unless it's being waved around like a sparkler; you see the tops of heads, not faces, and it's hard to distinguish children from adults. Drone pilots working off video feeds have accidentally targeted small children, old people, American troops, and American hostages. In the 1.2 seconds it takes the missile to travel from the drone to the ground, children have walked into the line of fire. After these experiences, the drone operator goes home to his or her family, admires a picture drawn at school, complains about traffic.

In February 2015, ISIS militants locked in a cage a twenty-two-year-old Jordanian pilot, soaked him in gasoline, touched torch to fuel, and filmed him as he slowly burned alive. Reality was deeply upset, and full of fury, as she often was, for the Islamic State, which she called IS. "Getting out of work," she wrote in an email to Golden, "I felt such a rush of emotion that I had been suppressing throughout the shift. I could not escape, or allow myself to put aside thoughts about the Jordanian pilot . . . I spent hours looking through all the latest reports . . . Wanting to find IS members became my witch hunt for the night. I spent hours playing mental chess with the world, who should strike first, hardest, what message should be sent, revenge, etc. . . . So on all fronts I just felt really helpless and overwhelmed. Naturally my thoughts had turned to yoga, because it is the means by which I can really understand and acknowledge powerful emotions and put them aside to gain more clarity and peace. But I didn't want to just hide in asana and meditation because it made me feel good. In the pain I felt, I did not want the 'moral' to be compassion and forgiveness."

Golden hadn't heard about the pilot. "I had to google it," he told me, "because I don't really follow the news."

She started dating a married man. He quickly became obsessed. She broke up with him, but she was upset and unsettled. A man she dated for a month woke Reality in the middle of the night; she kept making the same sound over and over. He repeated the sound for her. It was Pashto. The words for *mass grave*.

Reality's favorite part of the job was what she called "saving lives," but this intimate violence was not the way she wanted to save them. She wanted to do something humanitarian, and directly so. She was twenty-four years old. In her daydreams, Reality passed shoeboxes full of toys to children in refugee camps in a war-torn country on Christmas morning. She knew that this was not realistic, not what was needed; and she treated this dream with a wry, self-deprecating lightness. She gave what was actually needed: money to the Red Cross. She went back to work transcribing the tapped communications of suspected militants 7,000 miles away.

Once, when the girls were small, Billie and Ron had taken them to SeaWorld. They took in a show, watched sleek gray dolphins leap in unison, their sweet-sounding squeals elicited on command. Brittany was loving it. At which point her little sister—ever the explainer, ever the scold—declared that in captivity, the dolphins' signals bounce crazily off the walls; their capacity for echolocation drives them mad. For Brittany, the show was ruined. It had been easier not to know what was hidden below the visible, beneath the bright surface of the cage.

YOU DON'T HAVE THAT MANY

Prior to 2004, when reports about torture began to percolate in the press and among groups like Human Rights Watch, almost no one knew the term *waterboard,* a phrase which, oddly, centers the table onto which the man being tortured is strapped. It has been argued that the term *waterboarding* is actually a joke; a play on "surfboard." A better phrase would be *simulated drowning,* but even this doesn't really bring it across, because it is hard to imagine the kind of panic that takes over when your body believes that it is drowning. Men who feel that they are drowning break bones trying to free themselves from restraints. They convulse and vomit and weep. Their lungs can be permanently damaged, as can their brains. But by 2007 *waterboarding* was just a word, and the focus had not been on the subjective experience of Abu Zubaydah, a man who endured far more than simulated drowning, but on a debate over categories: Was waterboarding torture? If it was a secret that the U.S. poured water onto the faces of men it had strapped down, it was an open one. And yet as of 2007 no current or former U.S. official had confirmed, publicly, that this was the case.

Kiriakou had retired from the agency; he was now a well-paid corporate spy at Deloitte, for whom he tried to steal pricing models from other companies. He had also been, for a long while, a source on important stories investigative journalists were doing on the CIA. One of those journalists was ABC's Richard Esposito, an old-school journalist with a thick New York accent, who had been celebrated with Emmys and shared Pulitzers and Peabodys. In 2007, Esposito asked Kiriakou to go on the record and finally say something definitive about waterboarding from the perspective of a CIA veteran. Kiriakou says that Esposito used "an old reporter's trick" on him, implying that Kiriakou had been accused of complicity in torture and was free to come on the air and defend himself. Esposito says he was completely transparent about the risks.

Brian Ross is a deep-voiced anchorman you've seen before, but whose name you don't remember, so fully does he embody the role of messenger; in 2007 he was a fifty-nine-year-old white male, properly weathered, the invisible vessel through which passes news. In a basement studio in D.C., with one camera pointed at him and another at Kiriakou, Ross began asking questions about Abu Zubaydah.

"Why were you focused on him?" Ross asked.

"He was one of the financiers of the September 11th attacks," said Kiriakou, dressed in a suit jacket and purple tie; conservative, but not quite invisible. He was up against a bookcase, and when the segment finally aired the next day, it read EXCLUSIVE right over the top of his head.

"He was a—a logistics chief—of Al Qaeda," said Kiriakou. "And we knew that he was close to Bin Laden." His voice was sad and slow, as if delivering disappointing news to a child.

"He was unwilling to give us any actionable intelligence,"

Kiriakou said. "We had these trained interrogators who were sent to his location—to use the enhanced techniques as necessary to get him to open up."

"And can you describe them?" asked Ross.

What happens now depends on which Kiriakou you ask. Shortly after the interview, he would say he had no idea what he had walked into. That everyone knew this was the case anyway. Wasn't he just describing what had been in the press?

"In—in generalities," said Kiriakou, "I suppose I can say that—that my understanding is that what's been reported in the press—has been correct in that these enhanced techniques included everything from—what was called an 'attention shake,' where you grab the person by their lapels and shake them. All the way up to the other end, which was waterboarding."

"And that was one of the techniques."

"Waterboarding was one of the techniques, yes."

There had always been something in Kiriakou that made it hard for him to hedge. Another man would have said, "I can't confirm that, but it has been reported in the press." Another man might have pointed out that he, personally, had never witnessed torture, which was true. Ross was surprised by the candor.

"And was it used on Zubaydah?"

"It was."

"And was it successful?"

"It was."

"What happened as a result of that?"

"He was able to withstand the waterboarding for quite some time. And by that I mean probably thirty, thirty-five seconds—which was quite some time. And a short time afterwards, in the next day or so, he told his interrogator that Allah had visited him in his cell during the night and told him to cooperate . . . And from that day on he answered every question just like I'm sitting here speaking to you."

Ross's approach was gentle, not adversarial; he wanted his source to keep going.

"So your view was that waterboarding broke him."

"I think it did, yes."

"And did it make a difference in terms of—"

"It did. The threat information that he provided disrupted a number of attacks, maybe dozens of attacks."

"No doubt about that?"

"No doubt."

As the first former member of the CIA to acknowledge that the organization waterboarded detainees, Kiriakou was suddenly in great demand—on MSNBC, CBS, NPR. CNN called him "the man of the hour." Rush Limbaugh and Jonah Goldberg declared that the debate was over: Waterboarding worked. "Like flipping a switch," he had said. The next morning Dana Perino, the White House press secretary, wanted to talk about storms in the Midwest, but that was not what journalists were interested in discussing.

"Did the questioning of Al Qaeda leader Abu Zubaydah conform with the interrogation program approved by President Bush?" asked a journalist.

"I can't comment on any specifics," said Perino, flanked by large flags.

"I'm asking if it was within the guidelines, the interrogation techniques . . ."

"I will say that . . . the entire program has been legal."

"Are you saying that whatever was done in this case was not torture?"

"I am saying that the United States does not torture."

"But when you have a former CIA officer, John Kiriakou, now saying that waterboarding was used—since you're saying the interrogations were legal, he's saying on the record now, waterboarding was used . . . you're saying waterboarding is legal?"

"I'm not commenting on that gentleman's characterizations of any specific techniques."

"You just said it was legal."

"Yes."

"Everything that was done."

"Yes."

"So waterboarding is legal."

"I'm not commenting on any specific techniques."

There is no reason to doubt that Kiriakou believed what he said to Brian Ross—he based his information on "CIA cable traffic"—but almost nothing he said regarding the torture of Abu Zubaydah turned out to be true. Kiriakou was asked to do many more on-the-record interviews on the subject, and Esposito says he suggested he not do them. To do so could provoke retaliation, prosecution. Kiriakou kept talking. Soon after that, in the midst of the ensuing controversy, Kiriakou lost his job at Deloitte.

If you ask the Department of Justice, no one was ever prosecuted for the crime of admitting that the CIA had tortured Abu Zubaydah, though that would turn out to be a matter of opinion.

Leaks are the way Washington, D.C., communicates with itself. The fortress allows itself to be breached. The ship of state, the saying goes, is the only ship that leaks from the top. A leak is a way to draw attention, a method by which a career bureaucrat at the Minerals Management Service might communicate that a political appointee at the top is not paying sufficient attention to the safety of bowhead whales. Emails in which bowhead whale wellness is ignored become useful once public. Leaks are, according to one study conducted in the '80s, "a routine and accepted part of the policy-making process," unremarkable, boring, almost always unprosecuted. Forty-two percent of government officials surveyed for the paper said they themselves had leaked something, probably an undercount, which suggests that sharing classified information is just part of the job.

Informal leaks are informally addressed; leakers are frozen out of meetings, banished to other units. Kiriakou recalls a woman with whom he worked at the CIA who was sleeping with a reporter and gave up some classified info and was, as a result, suspended for two weeks. It was not until the Obama administration that the federal government seemed to have any real appetite for sending a leaker to prison. This is in part because the people leaking were not the right people. They were not, as one scholar put it, "legitimate participants in the game of leaks."

To the question of why the Obama administration prosecuted more leakers than all other administrations combined, and did so after a campaign focused on "transparency," is an open one. In an interview with *The New York Times,* a former DOJ spokesperson who worked under Bush professed to be "sort of shocked" by the volume of cases. "On balance," he told the *Times,* in what may or may not have been trolling the other party, "it is more important that the media have the ability to report. It's important to our democracy." The Obama administration said it went after leakers because it could win. "As a general matter," an unnamed official said, "prosecutions of those who leaked classified information to reporters have been rare, due, in part, to the inherent challenges involved in identifying the person responsible for the illegal disclosure and in compiling the evidence necessary to prove it beyond a reasonable doubt." Now there were emails to subpoena, texts to call up. They had the receipts.

In the SCIF on the basketball court Chelsea Manning opened a CD labeled LADY GAGA and downloaded hundreds of thousands of documents. She downloaded the video in which men with cameras were taken to be men with guns. While back home on leave, she sent it all to WikiLeaks via the anonymizing tool Tor.

Julian Assange was not a legitimate participant. He was not even American. As a young boy he'd lived on a small island off the northeast coast of Australia, among koalas, giant clams, rock wallabies, and hippies who slept on beaches. His mother called the move "going native." She married a theater director, Brett Assange. She herself was a puppeteer. They went on tour. Julian watched his parents put on small theatrical productions, pack up, and put them on somewhere else. They moved into an abandoned pineapple farm so thick with vegetation his mother got a machete and slashed her way to the front door. They moved to New South Wales. There were homemade puppets hanging from his bedroom window. Over the course of his childhood he attended thirty-seven different schools.

His mother left Brett. She married and had a second child

with a man named Keith Hamilton, whom Julian later said had fabricated his identity. Hamilton belonged to the Santiketam Park Association, which the *Sydney Morning Herald* calls "Australia's most notorious cult." The sect revolved around a woman who said she was Jesus reincarnated. Children were raised collectively believing she was their mother and allegedly subject to beatings. Julian's mother tried to leave Hamilton, but he wanted custody of their child. They ran from him—to Melbourne, Adelaide, Perth—packing up whenever he found them. They had been performers; now they lived in hiding. One should be careful in leaning too hard on the events of a childhood, but everything that came next could be explained by a boy split between spectacle and secrecy.

Julian Assange fathered a child and, as they say, learned to code. By the age of twenty he was a single dad and Australia's best hacker. He hacked into the Pentagon and into Lockheed Martin. When he was arrested by Australian police in 1994, the prosecution called his motive "simply arrogance." They wanted jail time, but the defense leaned on his tragic childhood, and the judge merely charged him $2,100. Assange thought himself the victim of a horrific injustice. Injustice was probably his favorite subject. "The more secretive or unjust an organization is," he wrote on his blog, "the more leaks induce fear and paranoia in its leadership and planning coterie . . . mass leaking leaves them exquisitely vulnerable to those who seek to replace them with more open forms of governance." *Exquisitely vulnerable.* He was a romantic on a quest to free the world. "Every day you live your life you lose another day of life," he once said, during a period of time when he was being pursued by more than a dozen national and international entities.

"What's the risk of just sitting there? You just lost a day. You just died a day. You don't have that many."

By 2010 Assange had figured out that a list of links would not draw the world's attention. You needed a spectacle. A literal unveiling. The child of actors, the boy with the puppets, put on a show. He organized a press conference at the National Press Club, invited journalists, and presented the video of American soldiers killing two Reuters journalists and wounding two children. He gave it a name and that name reflected not a pretense of objectivity but a clear point of view: "Collateral Murder." He threw a George Orwell quote in. The video begins with text and still pictures of the dead. He's making the journalists wait. "The video has not been released . . . ," reads the text. "Until now."

The video was edited to track Saeed and Namir and their cameras, but it did not point out that some among the other men carried weapons—including a rocket-propelled grenade. In text beforehand, we learn about Saeed's grieving son, but not that the Americans had been shot at earlier in the same neighborhood, and thus had at least some reason to suspect that the men were not peacefully gathering. We do not learn that they were charged with clearing the neighborhood of anti-Iraqi forces with small arms.

"You have edited this tape," said Stephen Colbert, "and you have given it a title called 'Collateral Murder.' That's not leaking. That's a pure editorial."

"The promise we make to our sources," said Assange, "is that not only will we defend them through every means that we have available, but we will try and get the maximum political impact for the material they give us." WikiLeaks was no longer an objective clearinghouse, a list of links, an uncensorable Wikipedia. It was framed and targeted. It would remain so as it took aim at American political figures distasteful to Assange, to the elevation of a president who understood, like Assange, the centrality of spectacle.

No one knew, at the time, who had leaked "Collateral Murder." No one knew that there were a quarter million more documents on the way. There was not yet the phrase "deluge leak." There were deeply detailed accounts of the war in Afghanistan. There were deeply detailed accounts of the war in Iraq. There were 250,000 cables exposing private conversations between American diplomats. All of this was transported to Assange by Manning via the grace of Lady Gaga, beginning in February 2010. There was so much information that the journalists who eventually mined the dumps had to set up a room and write computer programs to find out how to filter it, to find meaning and stories within this overwhelming mass of incriminating private communication. Tech writer Evgeny Morozov called WikiLeaks a "media darling" and speculated that it might become a kind of matchmaker for low-level leaks, interested journalists, and NGOs with related causes. WikiLeaks was associated with transparency, the weak against the powerful, and it was not meaningfully partisan. Assange cleaved the populace not into left and right but into libertarians and institutionalists, hawks and pacifists, advocates of transparency and supporters of an impregnable state. Through Manning he created a new kind of leak not targeting toward a specific wrong but covering many wrongs, an increase in scope that mirrored the increase in surveillance itself. If the government would collect data massively and indiscriminately, data would be leaked massively and indiscriminately.

All of this—the cables and the logs—amounted to the biggest leak in American history, and it had not come from a cantankerous sixty-year-old man nearing retirement, fed up with bureaucracy. At the time Manning seemed like an anomaly, but she was, in fact, a harbinger, the new template for leakers disastrous to the largest-ever shadow government. The greatest danger to the national security state was now ideological, morally serious twentysomethings finding themselves as they sifted through secrets their younger selves had promised to keep. They didn't trust the bureaucracies they were in and didn't feel intimidated by a media that would have seemed far away, inaccessible, in a pre-internet age of three networks and thick newspapers. The media was comprised of accessible personalities an email away. After Manning would come Edward Snowden, Reality Winner, and Daniel Hale. None of them had hit thirty-one on the day they blew the whistle.

The most accessible personality, because the most persistent and ubiquitous and resistant to silence, was perhaps that of Glenn Greenwald, who was in 2012 a left-libertarian lawyer-turned-blogger. That was the year he received an email asking for his public encryption, or PGP, key. Though he wrote primarily about national security, Greenwald barely knew what this was. He was not technically sophisticated. He ignored the email. The correspondent then sent him video instructions, as if written for a child, on how to set it up. He ignored that too. "I mean, now I had to watch a fucking video?" Greenwald later told *Rolling Stone,* in perhaps his most relatable moment. The correspondent gave up. Six months later, Greenwald heard from Laura Poitras, the filmmaker documenting Assange. Poitras was on a terrorist watchlist the government would not acknowledge existed. She had been stopped at the border "probably fifty times," her notebooks seized, her devices confiscated, her credit cards taken, and so she had moved to Berlin, where she could move in and out free of harassment. The three—Poitras, Greenwald, and the PGP-insistent source, who was, of course, Edward Snowden—would soon meet up in Hong Kong.

In June 2013 Greenwald published, with a *Guardian* reporter who had also met with Snowden, a report on PRISM—a top secret program through which the NSA demanded and received access to the systems of Google, Facebook, Verizon, and other companies. The story was massive, it was based on an infinitesimal fraction of what Snowden had to give, and it infuriated Julian Assange, who wanted to be at the center of it, but was not.

Two thousand thirteen was also the year Moscow hosted the Miss Universe pageant. When the finalists were selected, the judges were surprised at the names; the set of contestants was different from the one they had chosen. The pageant's owner, Donald Trump, had intervened. Some people said he chose women from countries in which he had business interests, and others say he tried to exclude women who seemed too "ethnic," though you could convince him to include an ethnic woman if she were a princess, or married to a football player. "Is Putin coming?" Trump asked throughout the pageant. Before the ceremony he had tweeted, "Do you think Putin will be going to The Miss Universe Pageant . . . if so, will he become my new best friend?" Trump sent him a personal invitation. Putin is "very interested in what we're doing here today," he told MSNBC. When Putin did not show, Trump floated the idea that he and his staff say he showed anyway, just for a little while. "I met him once," Trump said of Putin before the pageant, on Letterman, though that was not true.

The Obama administration revoked Snowden's passport and demanded he come home to face charges under the Espionage Act; instead, Snowden flew to Moscow, and it became popular to accuse him of being an agent of the Russian government. Senator Dianne Feinstein, Democrat of California, called the disclosures an act of treason, and John Boehner, Republican of Ohio, called him a traitor. John Bolton called it "the worst form of treason" and a senior fellow at the middle-of-the-road Brookings Institution published a piece called "Snowden's Treason" that took solace in the idea that maybe Putin would tire of Snowden and start treating him badly. More than half of Americans considered Snowden a whistleblower, but then it had been twelve years since 9/11, and most Americans were not heavily invested in the primacy of zero America.

James Clapper, the director of national intelligence, said the leaks did "huge, grave damage" but could not say what that damage was. Dick Cheney said he was possibly a spy for the Chinese. "When he emerged and when he absconded with all that material," said Hillary Clinton, "I was puzzled because we have all these protections for whistleblowers." If he were concerned and wanted to be part of the American debate, he could have been, she said. "But it struck me as—I just have to be honest with you—as sort of odd that he would flee to China, because Hong Kong is controlled by China, and that he would then go to Russia—two countries with which we have very difficult cyber-relationships, to put it mildly," a statement that elides the fact that a government hostile to the United States is the only kind that would not extradite him.

Billie Winner, Reality Winner's mother, thought Snowden was a traitor. In 2012 her daughter was at the military's language schools, learning the languages in which she would eavesdrop on enemies.

Greenwald spoke in complete, fluid sentences, arguing in an uninterrupted stream of purist logical abstraction; Assange's certainty, minus the sentimentality. He did not pepper his language with *to be sure*s or *the need to balance security and civil liberties,* and in refusing to do so, he denied to the secret state the deference a supposedly adversarial media had until now shown. "These systems," he told George Stephanopoulos, "allow analysts to listen to whatever emails they want, whatever telephone calls, browsing histories, Microsoft Word documents. It's an incredibly powerful and invasive tool exactly of the type Mr. Snowden described. NSA officials are going to be testifying before the Senate on Wednesday and I defy them to deny that these programs work exactly as I just said." He was accused repeatedly of aiding terrorists. "Nothing we exposed informed the terrorists of anything," he told filmmaker Morgan Spurlock. "We informed the American people that this spying apparatus built in the dark is aimed at them." He was perhaps most frequently told that if Edward Snowden had any honor at all, he'd come home and stand trial. "He's now gone to China and then to Russia," said Jeffrey Toobin on CNN, "and you don't think they now have access to all that material?" To which Greenwald responded, "No they don't, Jeffrey, and the reason he had to go to Russia and China is because the United States is filled with Jeffrey Toobins who want to take people who come forward and bring transparency to the government, and throw them into a cage for decades." (Toobin would later be undone by revealing his penis on a Zoom call, transparency in excess.) Michael Hayden called debating Greenwald "looking the devil in the eye."

"He's hiding in Russia!" said Paul Rieckhoff on *Real Time with Bill Maher*. "It would be a different story if he came back, and made his case, and faced the music. He could come back and make that case here on the show!" This was in 2014. Chelsea Manning was serving her sentence in a military prison in Kansas, during which she would not have the opportunity to appear on *Real Time with Bill Maher,* which is perhaps part of the reason why Snowden had accepted Julian Assange's help to find asylum in Russia.

In 2014 Laura Poitras, Glenn Greenwald, and journalist Jeremy Scahill founded *The Intercept,* an entire publication intended to analyze and exploit what former NSA and CIA director Michael Hayden called "the greatest hemorrhaging of legitimate American secrets in the history of the republic," funded by eBay billionaire Pierre Omidyar. "The Intercept Welcomes Whistleblowers" read its "become a source" page, offering instruction in transmitting documents securely. *The Intercept* reported, on the strength of an anonymous source who would turn out to be Daniel Hale, that the government was targeting people for assassination by drone using highly unreliable methods—mostly tracking them by cell phone, even though SIM cards were constantly traded—such that the wrong people were dying. They did so as Obama continued to maintain that the military used only extremely "precise" methods for assassination, "near certainty" that civilians wouldn't be killed, though hundreds already had been. *The Intercept* reported, on the strength of Snowden documents, that the NSA had plans to infect "millions" of computers with malware, and that it had disguised itself as a Facebook server to trick computers into accepting hacking tools. *The Intercept* reported that the NSA was archiving the audio of virtually every cell phone conversation in the Bahamas. After Hale printed it out at the National Geospatial Agency, *The Intercept* published the rule book for who gets put on the terrorist watchlist. *The Intercept* published the Drone Papers, also from Hale, which revealed that in a yearlong mission in Afghanistan, 200 people were killed by drone, only thirty-five of whom had been the intended targets. A leaker from within WikiLeaks leaked about WikiLeaks, and *The Intercept* reported.

All of this drama takes place in an age when U.S. intelligence agencies are having a lot of trouble with data. In this, they are relatable. This is a moment when we feel, as we gossip, the slightest twinge of anxiety that we've made of an unkind thought a reproducible record, that our friends will turn on us, that our phone will be lost and in the wrong hands found. This is a moment when a career in which we have invested can be undone by a stray thought shared prior to that career's launch.

In collapsing time the internet undoes the distance between ourselves and our past mistakes. A tweet from fifteen years ago has not yellowed and curled leaflike at the edges; it shimmers with the same fresh light as one you'll write tomorrow. We are all of us haunted because we live in this particular pocket of history in which we believe both in the internet and in the possibility of anonymity on that internet. We behave as if the network has no interest in us, and forget that interest may henceforth develop. This is a confusion about audience, and our temporal burden to bear.

This time collapse coincides with new powers of recall; with endless information comes the ability to take information from its context, to tell stories perfectly matched to the intentions of the teller, freed from the complex texture of reality. With endless information comes, of course, new possibilities of loss. It is not clear exactly when the NSA developed a powerful hacking tool called EternalBlue. We only know that by April 2017 it had lost control of it. A group calling itself the Shadow Brokers, thought by some to be backed by the Russian government, offered it up to the open internet. Various other groups of hackers, now empowered with weapons developed with the considerable capacities of the American state, then used EternalBlue to paralyze the city of Baltimore, German railroads, the British health-care system, among other entities. About this failure, the NSA mostly did not comment, and when former officials commented, the sentiments were defensive. "If Toyota makes pickup trucks and someone takes a pickup truck, welds an explosive device onto the front, crashes it through a perimeter and into a crowd of people," asked the former head of the NSA, who had been in charge when the door was left open, "is that Toyota's responsibility?" Historically, the National Security Agency does not excel at the act of taking responsibility in times of public failure, and nor, apparently, does it excel at analogies, but now it appeared to be even too much to expect that it would excel at national security.

The same year saw Vault 7, the leak of 9,000 pages of CIA documents detailing tools developed by the CIA, also at taxpayer expense. Here we find, made public, CIA-developed malware to infect Samsung TVs under the code name Weeping Angel, and to infect Windows under the sonically pleasing code name Brutal Kangaroo. The leaker made these public via WikiLeaks, rendering the tools useless.

There was also the president of the United States, himself a persistent threat to the sanctity of classified information, to which he was unrestrictedly privy, a subject that brings us, again, inevitably, to WikiLeaks, which after opposing for so long unaccountable American power suddenly found itself accused of being wedded to it.

On the part of the American intelligence agencies this had begun to look like assault. There was Assange, there was Snowden, there were *The Intercept*'s ever present personalities. All of these elements seemed designed to cultivate a kind of religiosity of transparency, a heroism accessible to the country's disgruntled insiders should they choose to join in the game of wanton exposure. They were lucid and smart and undeniably maverick. They were more knowable and yet more exotic than news anchors of the past; they offered a kind of imagined intimacy alongside the enduring romance of the outlaw.

To America's intelligence loyalists, this was a standing invitation to be used by well-funded forces bigger and smarter than you. If you shared American secrets, you shared them not just with Laura and Glenn and Julian; you shared with the enemy. Whether or not transparency was in the service of Americans themselves, this new, self-righteous world of celebrated dissidence was, to the NSA, essentially in the service of some foreign power that wished upon the United States chaos and humiliation, that sought to end American hegemony. Exactly which foreign power was being helped, and which was most eager to solicit and exploit the badly secured cache of American secrets in storage, remained vague until 2016, the year Donald Trump invited that country to hack into his opponent's emails.

Reality Winner had never gotten the war experience she had imagined, never worked abroad, never had an air force job not tied to a screen, so she left. She was honorably discharged in November 2016, at which point she applied for jobs with NGOs in Afghanistan, hoping to use her Pashto not to eavesdrop but to talk to people—maybe refugees, maybe kids on Christmas morning. She was not thinking about revolt, really. She wanted to change things from within. She read Madeleine Albright's memoir; she formed sober ideas about slow lasting change.

Reality's nonmilitary education stopped at high school, which is perhaps why her applications went nowhere. "They want a degree to hand out blankets," she told her mother. She was one of an infinitesimal number of Americans fluent in multiple Afghan languages, and yet she could not find a way to get out of an American office park.

During her years in the air force, Reality had, for a time, deployed to Fort Gordon, a base near Augusta, Georgia. After she was discharged, she got in her boxy, bumper sticker–covered Nissan Cube (ADOPT! / MAKE AMERICA GREEN AGAIN! / YOU JUST GOT PASSED BY A TOASTER), packed her belongings—which included an AR-15, a Glock, and a shotgun—and moved back. She taught at a CrossFit place, a high-end boutique gym, and a yoga studio while she tried to find a way to go abroad. Her days were structured by workouts. Sundays, Mondays, and Thursdays were her favorite days, because those days she lifted the heaviest weights at a bodybuilding gym, and did the best job of not thinking about the ongoing starvation in Yemen or the destruction of Aleppo, and the fact that there had been a city, and then there wasn't a city, and it was as if no one around her noticed at all. It wasn't that she didn't know she was coping with anxiety by overworking her body. She knew precisely what she suffered and what held it at bay.

Months passed. She downloaded the Tor Browser, curious about WikiLeaks, about how it all worked. She opened it up at a Starbucks, was underwhelmed, closed the window.

Reality did not have a college degree, but she was one of 1.4 million Americans with top secret clearance, which is to say that she had something to sell. Contractors are called body shops, and the bodies they want are security-cleared, readily found on sites like clearedconnections.com, which Reality frequented. Augusta was full of contractors paying good money for cleared linguists, and, unable to find something more appealing, Reality accepted a job with Pluribus International, a small operation owned by the son of a former CIA operative.

To get to the second floor of the Whitelaw Building, where Reality Winner appears to have worked from February until June, she first had to drive into Fort Gordon, HOME OF THE U.S. CYBER CENTER OF EXCELLENCE, past low-slung brick buildings and uniformed military in formation, past massive satellite dishes behind barbed wire, toward the $286 million, 604,000-square-foot sleek white listening post that is NSA Georgia, gleaming and gently curved, surrounded by a parking lot full of the middle-class cars of working intelligence-industry professionals.

"What do insider threats look like?" asks a student guide prepared by the Center for Development of Security Excellence. "They look like you and me."

Materials used for this training encourage employees to look out for coworkers who "display a general lack of respect for the United States." The phrase *way of life* comes up frequently, as in "Through unauthorized disclosures, we all risk losing our way of life" and "When you protect classified information you are protecting our nation's security, along with the warfighters who defend our American way of life." On a poster distributed by the CDSE, an American flag melts red and white over the words EVERY LEAK MAKES US WEAK.

Reality characterized her own insider threat training as "five hours of an SSO bitching about Snowden."

"I have to take a polygraph test where they're going to ask if I plotted against the government," she messaged her sister. "#gonnafail."

"Lol! Just convince yourself you are writing a novel."

"Look I only say I hate America three times a day. I'm no radical."

Reality was searched daily as she walked into the Whitelaw Building; more than once, Security commented on her health-conscious selection of lunch foods. The job, to the extent that there was a job, involved translating Farsi in documents relating to Iran's aerospace program, but no one in the building seemed to know what precisely she was supposed to do all day. She had a supervisor who was cleared to be on her floor, but her supervisor did not speak Farsi and couldn't engage with what she was doing. Lots of people seemed to have lots of extra time on their hands. Weekly, one gray-haired woman brought a two-pound bag of Tootsie Rolls to the office, unwrapped the candy, formed it into sculptures that resembled the poop emoji, and left them on random desks. At her own desk, Reality chatted with her old friends from the air force or watched neurology lectures on YouTube.

Thusly bored, with hours to kill every day, she searched documents well outside her area of expertise. She had access, for example, to a five-page classified report detailing a Russia-directed cyberattack on an American software company. According to the analysis, Russian intelligence sent phishing emails to the employees of the company, which provides election support to eight states, and got log-in credentials from someone. The Russians then sent emails infected with malware to over a hundred election officials, days before the election, from what looked like the software company's address.

The fall before she started at Pluribus, Reality and a boyfriend stopped seeing one another. In November, a man Reality referred to as "orange fascist" became president of the United States. Four days before Christmas, her father died. Though she kept it to herself at the time, she would later tell her sister that she would cry for thirty minutes a day, every day, during the weeks after his death. ("That sounds like Reality," her ex-boyfriend said when he heard this. "She would give herself exactly thirty minutes.") "I lost my confidant," she later wrote in a letter, "someone who believed in me, my anger, my heartbreak, my life-force. It was always us against the world. . . . It was Christmastime and I had to go running to cry to hide it from the family. 2016 was the year I got really good at crying and running."

It bothered her that the screens at NSA Georgia were always tuned to Fox News, and it bothered her enough that she filed a formal complaint. In her free time, she sought out the staff of Georgia senator David Perdue and arranged a thirty-minute meeting to discuss climate change and the Dakota Access Pipeline. On Facebook, she explained that she had drawn for Perdue's staff "a parallel between the

2011 interview of President Bashar al Assad claiming utter ignorance of the human rights violations his citizens were protesting" and Trump's claim that the White House had received no calls about the Dakota Access Pipeline. In April, the United States debuted its largest conventional weapon, known as MOAB (Massive Ordnance Air Blast bomb but also, commonly, Mother of All Bombs). It was dropped on Afghanistan, for what seemed to Reality to be no good reason, and in the United States, no one appeared to notice.

The document was marked TOP SECRET, which is supposed to mean that its disclosure could "reasonably be expected" to cause "exceptionally grave danger" to the United States, but then, of course, everything is classified. She had seen the question of whether the Russians were trying to take down American democracy bandied back and forth and back and forth, and it seemed to her that this specific account ought to be a matter of public discourse. "Russian General Staff Main Intelligence Directorate actors," it read, "executed cyber espionage operations against a named US company in August 2016, evidently to obtain information on elections-related software and hardware solutions." It was an account of the hacking of Florida-based VR Systems, of which the FBI had probably only told the White House, which was too cautious to share it, and Florida officials, where it was passively characterized as a "malicious act."

"There is a tremendous amount of hysterics, a lot of theories, a lot of premature conclusions being drawn around all of this Russia stuff," Jeremy Scahill had said on *The Intercept*'s podcast in March. "And there's not a lot of hard evidence to back it up. There may be evidence, but it's not here yet."

There was evidence available to Reality.

Why isn't this getting out there? she thought. *Why can't this be public?* Behind this was a building frustration with the way information had been disseminated since January 2017, when Trump had taken office. Each week there was a new scandal, each week mainstream media reported some misdeed and conservative media denied its import; each week Congress did nothing at all. What would they do with this? It seemed hard, definitive, in a way that a lot of that other stuff seemed soft; it seemed more difficult to disappear. Would anyone respond by increasing election security? Was the integrity of democratic votes an issue on which media factions could find a truce? People in dysfunctional relationships frequently devise tests for one another. Reality was devising a test for the United States.

This classified report on the Russian cyberattack was not a document for which Reality had a "need to know," which is to say she wasn't supposed to be reading it in her spare time, let alone printing it. Were she to print it, she was required to place it in a white slatted box called a "burn bag." But it was a document that she felt ought to be public. She was surprised that it had not already been leaked. She knew there were risks; for instance, she might get caught and have to take another training. She might even be fired.

"That day, that week," Reality said, "it was just too much, and to just sit back and watch it and think, *Why do I have this job if I'm just going to sit back and be helpless?*"

She landed on a web page—"The Intercept Welcomes Whistleblowers"—that included a SecureDrop link and physical addresses for *The Intercept* in D.C. and New York. She folded up the document, stuffed it in her pantyhose, walked out of the building. She left the document in her car; later that day, President Trump fired James Comey, who had been leading an investigation into Russian election-meddling, which intensified the perception that Trump had been helped by the Russians, and was afraid of exposure.

Two days later Reality placed the document in an envelope without a return address and dropped it in a standing mailbox in a strip mall parking lot.

TEN
PUPPIES

One of Joseph Biggs's tattoos said WAR and another said KILL, but he wasn't entirely clear whose bidding he was doing by killing these particular people in this particular war. As a kid in South Carolina, Biggs had been among the people who signed up out of anger over 9/11. It was confusing to him that he had then been sent to fight a war in Iraq, but then he tried not to think too much about it. "I just don't give a shit" is how he later characterizes his cast of mind. "My dick is hard. I want to fucking fight." He was thickset and short, an immovable object of a man, and this was how he always spoke, as if to assure the listener of a fearless solidity. He was coarse and puppyish, at once eager to offend and to be liked; in the kind of friends he had, these converged.

There was in Biggs a kind of persistent skepticism, an anti-authoritarian impulse looking to latch onto a story deeper than the story he had been told. He would never be good at accepting the official narrative; in this case, that he had been sent to Iraq to "keep America safe." Another story presented itself; it was called *Loose Change*. *Loose Change* was a documentary entirely comprised of evidence that 9/11 had been staged by the Bush administration. The film gave structure to the doubts of Biggs and many others. Biggs believed it, though believing his service was largely premised on lies had, in practice, little to do with his day job. He loved the men in his unit more than he did his own family. He was good at protecting them, regardless of why they were there. He would win a Purple Heart, be promoted to sergeant.

After Iraq, he was deployed to Afghanistan to fight the men with whom John Lindh had fought. In Afghanistan, in the service of stopping a second attack, Joseph Biggs, "balls deep in combat," "killed a bunch of Taliban." Afterward he and a friend were given a handheld device the size of a camera and told to roam the battlefield and scan the eyeballs of Taliban Americans had killed. All of the biometric information was sent from the device in Biggs's hand to West Virginia, where it was stored and presumably classified. It was important to Biggs's self-conception that this experience was something he could handle, and it seemed, for a while, that he could handle it, though the friend would descend into addiction. Biggs was sent to Fort Bragg, and all seemed well because he was still within the context that mattered, his unit. It wasn't until 2009, when the army sent him to El Paso, where he had no family, chosen or otherwise, that Biggs began to lose himself. In El Paso he was "alone with his own thoughts" and if he wanted to think about his old friends he would think about combat, which he "doesn't dwell on," and yet, in 2009, he began to wake from sleep weeping and screaming, believing that he was paralyzed. He began to drink nearly a bottle of tequila a day. Once he took a full bottle of sleeping pills, chugged tequila, hopped over the concrete wall in his backyard, and walked out into the open desert, where he hoped to die. When he was woken up in the hospital a senior commander asked if he had tried to kill himself. Biggs said he had not. He was at work the next morning. At a red light, he punched his steering wheel and wounded his fingers so badly one was scarred. He punched the roof of the car and left knuckle prints in the foam. He was medically discharged in 2009.

A year later, Julian Assange made an appearance in Stockholm. He had by this time grown to be a star of the hacker community, a group of people renowned neither for their social skills nor wokeness with regard to women. A Swedish journalist called him "a rock star . . . the majority of women who come in contact with him fall completely. They're bewitched." The activist who had invited him to Sweden to give a seminar invited him to stay in her flat. She was a thirty-one-year-old feminist named Anna who had started a queer nightclub, been an "equality officer" at a university, and said she would be away until Saturday, leaving him the apartment. But Anna came back a day early, on Friday, to the apartment with one room and one bed. He became aggressive, pulled off her clothes and snapped her necklace. She allowed him to take off her clothes, she says, blaming herself for initiating this. But she did not want to have unprotected sex, which he appeared to be forcing on her, holding down her arms and legs. He asked what she was reaching for; she said a condom. He put it on. But somehow, in the end, the condom was ripped, and he ejaculated inside of her. She thinks he did it on purpose.

She went to his lecture the next day, and when he said he wanted to try Swedish crayfish, she arranged a party at her house where he could have some. That day he met another woman, an as-yet-anonymous twenty-five-year-old who was a little obsessed with Assange, and had heard about

Anna's party. She was one of the first to sign up for the lecture, asked to be invited to lunch with the group. "He looked at me!" she texted a friend. At lunch she asked if he liked his meal, and he fed her a bite. They exchanged numbers. Later on during his stay in Stockholm, he invited her to meet him at night, after a meeting. They took the train back to her apartment, which was fifty miles away, but by the time they arrived their interest in one another had cooled. Assange fell asleep in her bed. During the night, they woke up and had sex. Assange complained that she insisted on a condom. After she made him breakfast, they had sex and fell asleep. The twenty-five-year-old says she woke to find that Assange was inside of her. "Are you wearing anything?" she asked.

"You."

He went back to the first woman's apartment, where he allegedly took off his clothes and began rubbing with his penis the thirty-one-year-old activist. She says she asked him to leave her flat, and he would not.

The next day, the twenty-five-year-old texted Anna. They compared notes. Anna said she would accompany the twenty-five-year-old to the police to report a rape, as moral support. But eventually her own accusations became part of the charges. When they asked Assange to take an HIV test, he refused, then relented, but by then it was the weekend and the clinics had closed. He left the country for England, but England ruled he must be extradited to Sweden to face questioning. Assange argued that it was a "honeytrap" operation set up by the CIA, though one imagines a honeytrap operation would be cleaner; he called Sweden "the Saudi Arabia of fundamentalist feminism." On Facebook, his twenty-one-year-old son Daniel said it would be "interesting" to find out whether the charges had been part of "a government plot or personal grudges," which indeed it would. "The man does have a way of making a lot of female enemies," he said.

In a documentary filmed by Laura Poitras, a polished, gray-haired lawyer named Helena Kennedy in a plaid blazer and turquoise necklace comes to talk to Assange about managing public relations as these accusations become public. They are on the British estate where Assange has set up base.

"It's about you getting your mind into not using language that sounds hostile to women," she says gently. "You have to find the language that helps you to explain that, other than sounding as somebody who thinks this is all a mad, um, feminist conspiracy. I don't think that's helpful to you."

"No," he says, tensing his shoulders, "to say it publicly it's not helpful."

"I know," she says, chuckling, "but I'd like to persuade you that it isn't true as well!"

"Privately," he says, "it's just a thoroughly tawdry radical feminist political positioning thing."

"And you've stumbled into this nest," she says, laughing, "of—! of—!"

"Yes! She started the lesbian nightclub in Gothenburg."

"People would say, what has her setting up a lesbian nightclub got to do with the price of fish?"

"She's in that circle," he says.

Kennedy stops laughing, purses her lips, and looks away into the distance.

Throughout this period, pursued by Swedish prosecutors and fearing that if he showed up for charges he would be extradited to the United States, Julian Assange was granted asylum in the Ecuadorean embassy in London. He arrived on a motorcycle disguised as a delivery boy and lived his days in the 330 square feet of what was not technically a prison. As a condition of his asylum, he had promised not to interfere in the politics of other nations, though he would in fact go on to contribute to the destabilization of the most powerful country in the history of the world.

Lady Gaga came to visit.

"It's like you're in college!" she said. "This is your room?!" She covered her eyes in exasperation.

She looked at his suit. "You should be in a dirty fucking T-shirt like a rebel, not in that suit." Assange took off his suit jacket.

Gaga herself was dressed in a high-necked, long-sleeved ruffled black dress and a giant white-brimmed black hat. She sat in an armchair and held a small camera aloft, interviewing Assange. Assange sat legs crossed, in a rumpled white T-shirt and socks.

"What's your favorite kind of food?" Gaga asked.

"Well, I went to Malaysia. Well first of all," he says, pointing his finger, "let's not pretend for a moment that I'm a normal person. I am obsessed with our political struggle. I'm not a normal person."

"I just would really like for you to tell me how you feel," says Gaga. "Because I've been trying to get that out of you—"

"But, OKAY, what does it matter how I feel? I mean who gives a damn? I don't care how I feel."

Gaga stares, impassive and increasingly frustrated, through the lens of her little camera.

"Do you ever feel like fucking crying?"

"No."

"You love your mom?"

"Yes."

By now Gaga has slumped into the armchair, almost sulking, under the black halo of the wide-brimmed hat.

"How about your dad?"

"My dad is much more abstract, so . . ."

"No! Nothing like you then!" She laughs.

He was, by all accounts, a terrible houseguest. He had a cat named James he refused to feed or clean up after. At night, he skateboarded through the rooms. His room smelled. He accused the embassy staff of spying for the Americans, and he paraded around the cramped embassy wearing only his underwear. Once, he got so angry at the staff that he smeared his own feces on the embassy walls. One could be forgiven for wondering, reading these reports, whether it was past time Assange, stuck for year after year in the place that was not a jail, started caring about how he feels. It would turn out to be extremely unfortunate for enemies of state surveillance that one of their greatest allies did not, over ten days in Sweden, want to use a condom.

The way the law came for John Kiriakou was both dizzyingly complex and narratively simple, a tale straight out of Kafka, in that the characters were familiar and the law clear but the sudden decision to enforce that law went deep into questions of norms and ethics and the technology coming for us all. It was 2012, more than a decade after he'd helped chase down Zubaydah, and five years after saying the word *waterboard* on ABC. He had made a lot of mistakes and which mistake mattered would be a subject taken up by the court. The way the law came, first, was via a Fox News van parked in front of his three-bedroom house in which he waited, sleepless, both because he had a newborn baby boy and because he had recently turned himself in to the FBI for charges that might land him in jail until the child was forty-five. He told Heather he wanted to kill himself, but Heather was firm and reassuring, good in a crisis. She didn't blame him for any of it. They had three kids and someone had to be strong. He had always been the emotional one. He was the one who would insist on a locus of blame, and that locus was a journalist named Matthew Cole.

Cole had been, at the time, employed by ABC News along with Richard Esposito and Brian Ross. He was a young journalist who liked to call himself "delusionally ambitious," and this appeared to be true in that he often had big ideas for stories he could not produce. But Cole was relentless and capable and he aimed his energy directly at the darkest corners of American power: secret prisons, torture, Blackwater. He had deep sources in secret places, not an easy thing to find in a reporter. He was good, according to a colleague, at "getting a certain kind of violent man to talk," a capability evinced in, say, a horrifying report on Navy SEALs desecrating the bodies of men they've killed by, among other things, "canoeing" their skulls in two. These are stories worthy of our admiration in part because they are stories no one wants.

That Cole's energy for discovery sometimes overwhelmed his conscientiousness became Kiriakou's problem, but not only his. Cole said his direction and sense of mission came to him, as with Reality Winner, via 9/11. He was at Columbia Journalism School at the time. He made his way to Afghanistan, and he broke news.

In 2008, the year after Kiriakou appeared on ABC in a purple tie and declared that waterboarding broke Abu Zubaydah, Matt Cole was working on a book about the CIA's 2003 abduction of an Egyptian man in Italy, a difficult book to report given the fact that key characters were undercover. Cole emailed Kiriakou, asking for names.

"Sorry Matt," Kiriakou said, "I never met any of those guys."

Cole kept trying. "Presumably, [first name]," he said, referring to a CIA operative.

"He had been my branch chief," responded Kiriakou, "but he's the only one I ever came into contact with."

"Presumably [first name] worked in that group though, right?" Cole asked.

"I assume he did," said Kiriakou. "He was the team leader."

A month later, Cole emailed Kiriakou with a list of names, asking him to pick out the last name of the man they'd been discussing. His last name was not on this list. The next day, Kiriakou responded with the first and last name. "It came to me last night," he said.

When Cole had the name, he wanted contact information, which would have potentially been available via LexisNexis. But Cole did not have access to LexisNexis. And so he gave the name given to him by Kiriakou to someone who did have LexisNexis: the director of a research firm named John Sifton.

"My guy came through with his memory," Cole wrote.

As it turned out, Sifton was somewhat of a specialist in tracking down deep cover CIA agents. He was doing so for the lawyers of men held at Guantánamo, compiling names of CIA agents who may have been responsible for abuse. He would send the lawyers, eventually, a document that included eighty-one names, and when, through the judicial process, it reached the CIA, the CIA considered the list itself potentially criminal. It filed a crimes report.

Matthew Cole had spoken to Kiriakou in 2008. It wasn't until 2012 that the FBI called Kiriakou asking for help on a case. "Could you come down here?" they asked. Unworried, he met them in a secure room at FBI headquarters in Northwest D.C. It was an hour into the interview, Kiriakou says, when he realized he was the target. The agents told him that "Officer A" had been revealed. "How the heck did they get him?" Kiriakou asked. That officer, he said, "was always undercover. His entire career was undercover." Had Kiriakou revealed the name? "Goodness, no.... Once they get the names, I mean this is scary." An agent said, "You should know we are executing a warrant on your house as we speak."

How did the FBI find out Kiriakou spilled the name? Kiriakou considered himself burned; in conversation with me, he called Cole "a fucking retard," though he also called him "very good-looking." Days after Kiriakou's prosecution went public, handsome Matthew Cole was no longer employed by ABC.

The charges amounted to a possible forty-five years in prison; what Kiriakou calls "a death sentence." He would not know his own children, one of whom was in utero. Heather was on maternity leave from her job at the CIA. The agency called with the news that she would have to resign, which did not surprise her. He thought about going to Home Depot to buy some spouting pipe to attach to his car's exhaust.

Kiriakou's best friend called early in the morning and said that a woman was quoted in a lot of articles about him. "I'm not reading any more articles about myself," Kiriakou said. Call her, said the friend.

John Kiriakou called Jesselyn Radack in her office. It wasn't yet 7:00 A.M.

"Oh my God!" she said. "How are you?"

"I'm going to kill myself today," he said. "I'm pretty confident that's what's going to happen today."

"No," she said, "no. Come to my office."

They met for hours; she agreed to help. "I want to especially thank you," Kiriakou said, "because I know that you specialize in whistleblower cases, and I'm not a whistleblower."

"But you are a whistleblower," Radack said.

"No. I just said something basically to protect myself."

"Listen," Radack said. "Whistleblowers have to be told that they're whistleblowers."

Whether or not Kiriakou was a whistleblower was complicated then and is more complicated now, but what is clear is that Radack took over Kiriakou's PR, and Radack knew how to frame a story. His attorneys had told him not to talk to the press. Jesselyn set him up with a half dozen interviews with well-known journalists in major publications. "That," says Kiriakou, "is when CNN stopped calling me 'CIA Leaker John Kiriakou' and started calling me 'CIA Whistleblower John Kiriakou.' "

His defense team, he says, hated her, hated the press. They were busy trying to get the case dismissed based on the doctrine of "selective prosecution," which is to say based on the idea that other leakers had not been prosecuted, and that Kiriakou had been singled out because he had embarrassed the government during the Brian Ross interview. "The only difference between those who have escaped prosecution and John Kiriakou is that the others leaked classified information with the tacit approval of the United States government, or revealed information the government considered favorable," they argued. They pointed to recent stories that depended heavily on classified leaks:

A *New Yorker* story on the raid that killed Osama bin Laden; a book about the search for Bin Laden; a *Washington Post* profile of the director of the CIA's Counterterrorism Center; an Associated Press story about a foiled Yemeni plot to blow up an American plane. "The one common element among these unprosecuted leaks," wrote the lawyers, "is that they portray the government in an excellent light." They claimed this prosecution was both selective and vindictive, a delayed response to the fact that Kiriakou had blown the whistle on torture.

To the prosecution this was absurd: Kiriakou had revealed the name of a covert officer to a reporter, lied about it to FBI agents, and retroactively claimed status as a whistleblower for an unrelated incident.

Kiriakou says he spent all he had on lawyers, and by October he owed them $880,000 more, and when he was out of money and the lawyers were out of ideas, he pled. All the charges except one—his communication with Cole—were thrown out. He was sentenced to thirty months, and at the hearing the judge wanted to make clear that Kiriakou's sentence had nothing to do with an embarrassed CIA.

"Mr. Trout," said Judge Leonie Brinkema, "the Court has great respect for you. I've always enjoyed having you in my court, but I must say your allocution did not ring well in my ears. This case is not a case about a whistleblower. It's a case about a man who betrayed a very solemn trust." She spoke of the life of the CIA agent, "changed forever," she said, though those details are classified and not available to us. "Thirty months," she added, "is frankly way too light."

"Mr. Kiriakou, come up to the lectern," said the judge. "This is your chance to say anything you'd like the Court to consider before sentence is imposed."

"Thank you," said Kiriakou. "No, Your Honor."

"All right," she said. "Perhaps you've already said too much."

Kiriakou was the first CIA officer ever to be convicted for a leak. CIA director David Petraeus called it an "important victory" for the intelligence community. "Oaths do matter," he went on, "and there are indeed consequences for those who believe they are above the laws that protect our fellow officers."

Two weeks later, FBI agents confronted a woman named Paula Broadwell, who had written a book called *All In: The Education of David Petraeus* and with whom Petraeus had had an extramarital affair. "Dangerous Dave," she had called him; also: "Peaches." In order to assist her with his biography, Petraeus had given her eight little black books of his own notes, each full of classified information; according to the indictment: "identities of covert officers, war strategy, intelligence capabilities and mechanisms, diplomatic discussions, quotes and deliberative discussions from high-level National Security Council meetings." There were emails from Petraeus to Broadwell detailing the fact that he knew precisely what he was doing. "They are highly classified," he had told her before handing them over. "I mean there's code word stuff in there." Petraeus was convicted of only a misdemeanor. He never served a day in jail. Soon after, he was a partner in a private equity firm, actively lobbying Donald Trump to name him secretary of state.

In court the withholding of classified information comprised a "sacred trust," and the sharing of it was the stuff of betrayal, of Hollywood, of great narrative turning points involving tight-lipped men and park benches and suitcases of secrets. But in practice the relationship with classified information would seem to be a casual one, even or especially to the director of the CIA, a man trusted with far more information than was ever available to John Kiriakou or certainly Reality Winner. *This is heavy stuff,* you say, *code word stuff,* as you hand over the goods. How else, in a world where seemingly all knowledge is classified, could a man communicate? You couldn't possibly function, couldn't do your job, if you didn't break rules every day.

But the law was the law, and the DOJ could decide when to apply it without fear, it turned out, that a judge would call that prosecution "selective," and so on an unusually warm February day John Kiriakou spent one last afternoon with his kids. The law was the law and so Kiriakou jumped on the trampoline and tried not to think about anything beyond the three of them. "I'm going to go to Pennsylvania for two years to help bad guys get their GED," he told his seven-year-old, a story that worked until a day when his son came to visit and saw his dad walk through a door that said INMATE and asked what that word meant and having thought about it for a terrible moment finally said, "So are you a teacher or are you a prisoner?"

Whether out of compulsion or economic necessity or both, Kiriakou simply never stopped talking. He took to the identity of whistleblower, relished in it. It gave him a platform from which to pronounce. From prison he published a column called "Letters from Loretto," which he then compiled for a book about prison, in which he describes correctional officers as "assholes, power-mad bullies, passive-aggressive instigators, all around dicks." He stayed informed and he had many opinions he was eager to express, on the pedophiles in lockup or sentencing reform or the courage of Edward Snowden. "They're trying to silence me," he writes in his book, but no one has succeeded in this. Jesselyn had gotten him a subscription to *The New York Times,* which was delivered to him in prison, and three months before he got out, he read an article on the Senate Intelligence Committee Report on Torture, which either vindicated him as a whistleblower or revealed the full extent of his self-deception, or both.

"And was it successful?" Brian Ross had asked that day in front of the bookcase before someone slapped the word EXCLUSIVE over Kiriakou's head. "It was," Kiriakou had said. And six years before that Kiriakou had said goodbye to Zubaydah in the dirty hospital with the Irish Spring. The men who took him from the hospital put a diaper on Zubaydah and a hood over his head. "It was clear to me that I was boarding a plane," Zubaydah wrote in his notes. He was shackled into an excruciating position on the plane for hours and hours, alongside other prisoners. He was relieved to feel the plane hit the ground, but once they had landed, he was shackled on the ground into an even more painful position. He remembers the sounds of vomiting, moaning; someone shouting, "My back! My back!"

Zubaydah was first interrogated by experienced FBI interrogators who held his hand as he recovered from injuries sustained during the raid. This was a traditional interrogation, like the one Reality would undergo, with the appearance of gentleness, the rapport-building. This is the interrogation that worked. But it was thought by the CIA that Zubaydah was hiding more. It was March 2002 and no one knew where Osama bin Laden was hiding and many, many people felt the United States had been too gentle, too focused on human rights, and so had become a victim of people with no such qualms.

The CIA did not have expertise in torture, because torture is illegal. What it had were two middle-aged psychologists, Bruce Jessen and James Mitchell, who had a narrow job within the air force's Survival, Evasion, Resistance, and Escape school: to help airmen who might be subjected to torture in rogue counties—the kind of countries that employed torture—to learn how to withstand it. That is to say, they had no expertise in the subject of how or whether torture might be used to extract true information. They were men who knew what waterboarding was, and how best to endure the feeling of being drowned, information they passed on in the unlikely event that anyone they trained would ever have to use it. In the words of the Senate Intelligence Committee Report on Torture, "Neither psychologist had any experience as an interrogator, nor did either have specialized knowledge of al-Qa'ida, a background in counterterrorism, or any relevant cultural or linguistic expertise." They didn't have expertise, or relevant scholarship, but they had some big ideas, some experiments they were eager to run. The architects of the CIA's torture program called themselves "Mitchell Jessen and Associates" and billed the CIA for $81 million.

If the point of prison is the erasure of context, then a secret prison is the best and highest fulfillment of the ideal. Zubaydah was in Thailand, but he could have been anywhere. He remembers waking up and finding himself chained to a steel bed, behind bars. He was in a white cell with no natural lights, four bright halogen lamps, and constant, pounding music—whatever CDs the guards happened to have with them. An FBI interrogator would later remember it being Red Hot Chili Peppers, a band to which he never listened again.

As Zubaydah began to fall asleep, he felt water on his face. He looked up and saw "a black object carrying a water tank." Eventually the object resolved itself into a man dressed in black, with black goggles and black fabric covering his face. Zubaydah tried to speak to him, but the music was too loud. Every time he closed his eyes, the figure in black would throw water on him.

The room had a white curtain separating the cell from the interrogation room, and, crucially, an air conditioner. Mostly, Zubaydah was naked. He was very cold, and the water thrown on him was colder. Sometimes he was fed nothing for days; other times, he was fed only Ensure and water for weeks at a time. All of the security officers wore black uniforms, including boots, gloves, balaclavas, and goggles, and for forty-seven days of isolation, prior to questioning, Abu Zubaydah saw only these faceless black-clad bodies. Abu Zubaydah had a bad memory; his diaries had been taken from him; he was now in a white room manned by men covered in black cloth. There was nothing here to trigger recollections of the life he had before. It was as if someone had instead designed a mechanism to suppress them. His mental map of the world went missing. Above him, in the cell, was a video camera, surveilling twenty-four hours a day, making a new one.

It is unclear for how long he was forced to stay awake in the windowless rooms with the halogen lamps, but the assistant attorney general at the time was assured no one would be kept awake "for more than eleven days."

"It felt like an eternity to the point that I found myself falling asleep despite the water being thrown at me by the guard who found himself with no choice but to strongly and constantly shake me in order to keep me awake," he writes, as if the guard, too, lacked agency. "Then I got used to the shaking just as I got used to the water being thrown at me, so I was able to sleep for a second." At which point an interrogator would come in and stand him on his feet. Sometimes, when he kept falling asleep, he was forced to walk on his wounded leg. He would fall.

Studies on sleep deprivation have a kind of primitive quality, such that we don't really know how much the human body can endure. "In 1984, a researcher kept ten puppies awake for 96 to 120 hours," notes a recent report on American torture. "The study ended because all of the puppies died."

One day in August 2002, men entered the cell, stripped him, shackled him, placed a hood over his head, placed a rolled towel around his neck, held on to the end of the towel, and slammed Zubaydah's naked body against the cell wall. They strapped him to a board and poured water on his face; he convulsed and vomited. They brought a "confinement box," meant to look like a coffin, into the room.

A medical officer sent an email back to Langley with the subject heading: "So it begins: The sessions accelerated rapidly progressing quickly to the water board after large box, walling, and small box periods." In August 2002, for a period of seventeen days, Abu Zubaydah was tortured twenty-four hours a day. They kept him standing and awake. During this period he was not alone, because a man had to stand next to him and douse him with cold water whenever he fell asleep. He spent a total of eleven days and two hours in a coffin-sized box.

But there was another box. This box would fit under your desk: a box with a width under 2 feet, a depth of 2.5 feet, and a height of 2.5 feet. Abu Zubaydah was put in this box for a total of twenty-nine hours. He begged and wept and whimpered. CIA personnel also cried. Zubaydah maintained, consistently, that he had no new information. He was strapped to a board and a tube was stuffed into his rectum. Sometimes, this is how he was fed. In the CIA report it is called "rectal rehydration," a sterile description, intended perhaps to sound medical, but medicine is the art of care, and this was its opposite.

Zubaydah was not subjected to the experience of drowning one time, as Kiriakou had said, but eighty-three times over seventeen days. The video camera recorded him vomiting and screaming.

Much later, when lawyers were trying to help Zubaydah recall how he had been treated, he was given a pad and black, blue, and red pens. Zubaydah began to draw, just as he had in his diaries. His drawings show great care and attention to detail. You can see spiral grooves on the neck of the bottle used to drip water into his mouth. The buckles used to strap him down. His legs are covered in hair; his shaved head and beard show black stubble. His body is naked and the anatomy is careful. There are wavy lines around his hands as he is drowning, tremors of pain. His mouth is a simple black hole, a small dark abyss at the center of the scene. In one picture he is being slammed against a wall, and sharp, angular red lines surround his throbbing head. In releasing these drawings, the CIA has placed a black box over the head of the person doing the slamming, as if the drawing would help identify him. It is a kind of compliment.

Eventually even Mitchell and Jessen, the psychologists-turned-torturers, wanted it to end. The CIA ordered them to keep going; the psychologists claim they were called "pussies" for wanting to stop. They refused to go on unless the CIA sent agents from Langley to observe what was happening. So CIA agents came to Bangkok to watch interrogators perform what they called a "perfunctory" version of the process.

By the end of the seventeen-day period, according to the torture report, an interrogator would walk into the room with the tilted board and the man it was for. The interrogator would raise an eyebrow. Seeing this, Zubaydah would slowly walk over to the board. The interrogator snapped his fingers twice. Zubaydah lay down on the board, and waited passively to be restrained. It is not clear whether, at any point during this period, Zubaydah realized he was in a secret American prison in Thailand.

The CIA told the National Security Council that torture was producing meaningful results, but this, as the Senate report details, was a lie. All of the useful information Zubaydah provided, he provided to the FBI, which did the normal, boring things one does in interrogations. "The use of the CIA's enhanced interrogation techniques was not an effective means of obtaining accurate information," concludes the Senate report. The psychiatrists would later argue that torture was useful because by providing no information under torture, Abu Zubaydah confirmed that he had no information.

In the 525 unclassified pages we have of the Senate Intelligence Report on Torture, there is no evidence of an earnest attempt to seek out historical or scientific research, or even serious theoretical work, on how best to extract useful information from a prisoner in a timely manner. There is merely trust in men who studied other things in graduate school (Mitchell studied the effects of diet and exercise on blood pressure; Jessen studied family therapy) who say they know what they are doing, and there is a billion-dollar agency that decides to believe them. These actions are so far from what an intelligent person would do if one's only aim was to extract information that it is hard to make sense of them absent the existence of a positive desire to torture. "It was the worst day we have ever seen," John Kerry once said of 9/11, "but it brought out the best in all of us."

Given this lack of interest in the boring and time-tested rapport-building interrogation techniques that produce good information, the CIA had made a mistake. Abu Zubaydah was not Osama bin Laden's deputy. He was not even a member of Al Qaeda. He was someone who had handled logistics at a training camp for fighters in Afghanistan in the '90s, involved in terrorism, yes, culpable, perhaps, but never privy to the information for which he was being repeatedly slammed against the wall.

Faith in country is a durable thing. A full five years later, well after the CIA had destroyed the tapes it had made of itself torturing Abu Zubaydah, this is what CIA veteran John Kiriakou told Brian Ross: This man was Al Qaeda's number three. Having been waterboarded once, he said Allah came to him in a dream and told him to confess, and "from that day on, answered every question." He gave answers that prevented "maybe dozens" of attacks. Like "flipping a switch." This is not just propaganda; it is torture fan fiction. It suggests not only a psychic need to torture but a need to frame it as an act of life-saving heroism. Fairy tales are stories in which darkness precedes transformation, and this is a story for America's children: We stuffed a man in a small box to set you free.

A VERY HARD CASE

It was inevitable that Reality would be seen through the lens of Snowden, who had also been very young, had also signed up for the military, through which he, like Reality, had first obtained security clearance, had also grown disillusioned, grown bored. He had worked in intelligence—the CIA—and then, as with Reality, become a contractor for private industry. Once, a slightly annoyed OB/GYN called me a "persistent self-advocate." Reality and Edward fit this description. When the CIA put up Snowden and other recruits at a decrepit Comfort Inn, he filed a formal complaint with the person in charge of the program. When he was ignored, he took the complaint to that person's boss. When that person's boss ignored him, he took it to *their* boss. He was reprimanded, but the trainees no longer had to stay at the Comfort Inn.

Snowden is a savant of the lucid explanation. What he is explaining is typically the relationship between secrecy and the state. He can speak for three straight hours making unimpeachably cogent points and never once express doubt or uncertainty, which has the effect of making him sound like a crank who is not so much removed from reality as unhealthily tethered to it. In the days he spent exploring the darkest corners of the NSA's capabilities, he found that every day the FBI handed over a CD to the NSA. On that CD were one billion American phone records. With those records, the NSA built what journalist Barton Gellman calls a "live, ever-updating social graph of the United States."

The NSA had the capacity to search for anyone and conjure a map of connections. A contact chain. It was more than static metadata, more than a list of links, because it expanded across time; having targeted someone, you could rewind. Yes, today you talked to the pediatric dermatologist with whom you share a political orientation, but now that we're interested—to whom did you both talk yesterday, and was it the ski instructor newly suspected of selling MDMA to parents at the Montessori school? It was, writes Gellman (who writes beautifully and thus will be quoted liberally), "a database that was preconfigured to map anyone's life at the touch of a button. . . . Our dossiers floated formlessly in a classified cloud, precomputed and untouched until someone asked for them." Snowden revealed that Google, Facebook, AOL, and others were knowingly funneling their users' data straight to the NSA; they unlocked the doors to loud rooms full of racks and wire so the NSA could come in and install equipment with which to spy.

The NSA could record live audio, live video, live chat. It could watch you type search terms into Google. It could monitor, if it chose, your very keystrokes. In theory the NSA was not allowed to spy on the citizens who paid taxes to fund it, but in practice, in targeting foreigners, it amassed endless data on Americans. They were part of the chain, "incidental" to it. Swept up, mostly from people who were not targets, were the ephemera of everyday life. Snowden gave Gellman access to some of them: "They told stories of love and heartbreak, illicit sexual liaisons, mental health crises, political and religious conversions, financial anxieties, and disappointed hopes. They included medical records sent from one family member to another, résumés from job hunters, and academic transcripts of schoolchildren. In one photo, a young girl in religious dress beamed at a camera outside a mosque. Scores of pictures showed infants and toddlers in bathtubs, on swings, sprawled on their backs, and kissed by their mothers. In some photos, men showed off their physiques. In others, women modeled lingerie."

I teach what has regrettably come to be called "creative nonfiction" to graduate students. Sometimes they write about forests and minds and the Beach Boys, but often they write about grotesque familial infighting, years of neglect and abuse, suffering at the hands of those they love. They write about their demons and the people they've wounded in trying to expel them. At the end of every semester, the question arises: How can I publish this in a world where people I love are literate? Implicit in this question is the assumption that it's okay to tell us, the workshoppers; we're strangers; at worst, acquaintances. How easy it is to confess to someone with whom you have no history. The internet's danger is that it presents itself as the stranger. I don't want my mother to follow my keystrokes, but Google's attention seems far less threatening. To think it would care invokes a kind of narcissism that doesn't, for most of us, come naturally.

Thusly we give more and more and more; searching is thinking. Extended across time, it becomes a record of thought more reliable than any diary entry. A day's entry in a journal is considered, framed. But there is no narrative perspective in a search, just the unspooling of a series of questions. Google has my searches. The NSA can ask for them. Either could thus see me, on a late night, spiraling: *colic solutions, baby won't stop crying, colic peer reviewed studies*. And later: *pediatrician colic, colic long-term effects, colic average duration*. And later: *foods breastfeeding colic*. And later: *anxiety drugs safe for breastfeeding*. And later: *adoption*. I didn't tell anyone beyond Google about this spiral. I'm only telling you now because I don't know you.

For weeks, Reality continued to go to work, to be thoroughly searched on her way in and way out. She repeatedly checked *The Intercept* but did not there find the document she had sent. Perhaps it had not been such a big deal. She taught a yoga class. She texted her sister. She was dealing with the messy end of another relationship. She was twenty-five years old and didn't know what she wanted to do with her life. She knew it was not this. What was she waiting for, exactly? Had her life started yet? She had joined the military so she would not be stuck in a classroom. She had spent six years locked down in offices, before screens. Her father had waited to go abroad, had spoken of the Mayan ruins, and had never made it. Last minute, Reality booked a trip to Belize.

The Snowden documents were treated, by *The Intercept*, with reverential safety protocols. To access them you had to enter a tiny room with a lock that required multiple people to open. You couldn't be in there alone. There were cameras everywhere. Everything logged. The computer itself was connected to nothing, air-gapped. This was something *The Intercept* had the capacity and expertise to do:

report on documents a savvy leaker had handed them in a responsible way. It was, frankly, a pain in the ass, so much so that some of the staff felt the documents were underused; there was interesting stuff that was just too annoying to report on. Others thought it was security theater, a kind of self-important, self-imposed performance. The world of the small locked room is the world we can imagine Reality envisioned when she posted the document, but the journey her document took bore no relation to this at all. It would involve different players, and different protocols, if you could call them that.

It started, as we said, with a P.O. box full of garbage. This was the P.O. box listed on the "Intercept Welcomes Whistleblowers" web page. It wasn't anything whistleblowers had heretofore used, and it wasn't often checked. When it was, the box was usually, according to one staffer, full of letters addressed to Greenwald or another reporter, Lee Fang. When, in May 2017, a staffer took the key to the box around the corner, he found a standard white envelope postmarked weeks ago in Augusta.

The staffer who worked on Russia stuff showed the document to another staffer and asked if she thought it was real. She thought it might be. He contacted Roger Hodge, the managing editor, who said to tell one of their national security reporters known to have sources in the intelligence community. This was, incredibly, Matthew Cole, who had come to work for *The Intercept* in 2015, months after Kiriakou had been released from prison. The story was also assigned to someone working at *The Intercept* on a contract basis, having been brought on for another story. This was Richard Esposito, the reporter who had gotten Kiriakou to go on the record about torture. The D.C. staffers put the document in a safe, and soon after, Cole and the publication's two top editors—Betsy Reed and Roger Hodge—took the train down to D.C. to retrieve it. For days, based on Cole's reporting, they wavered about whether the document was a hoax. There were reasons to believe it was a hoax, and there were reasons to take it seriously.

There was buzz in the open New York office. Some who were there at the time will tell you that it was a "big, important story," the biggest of the new editor's and the biggest of the assigned reporter's since coming onto the publication, that the office was abuzz with "something big," and others will tell you there was not an appropriate sense of urgency. Both appear to be true. Most people knew nothing about the document, but people knew something was up, to the extent that some reporters felt excluded. "I often feel," someone later said in an internal report, "that I am not asked."

Cole made, or was allowed to make, various mistakes in the handling of the document, though one could argue that the primary mistake was in assigning him the story. Here was a reporter not known to be especially digitally adept, who had not been involved with the intense security measures taken around Snowden. Here was someone usefully arrogant, confident enough to go after the CIA's secret network of prisons and succeed, and yet here was someone called not only "arrogant" but "sloppy" even by colleagues who profess to like him. (Cole disputes this characterization and stands by his work.)

There were people with deep knowledge of digital security available to anyone at *The Intercept*. Upon seeing such a document, they would have known that it contained subtle traces of its origins: in the creases, in the printer markings. They might have suggested retyping the document from scratch, generating new graphics to match the old. They would have known that the real challenge would have been authenticating the document without any knowledge of who sent it, and so they might have suggested describing it in only vague terms to the NSA, or avoiding the NSA altogether and using open source intelligence. They would have understood that this document, if real, involved profound risk to its human source and that—given the NSA's internal surveillance—there may have been no way at all to publish a story on it without endangering that source.

The central mystery here, unanswerable even by key players, is why no one asked for the security team's assistance. The team was not aware that Reality's document existed until after it was published. In internal interviews afterward, many members of the staff said they assumed that of course Security had already dealt with this. "At the time, I just assumed due diligence" had been done, said one person involved. "These were an experienced reporting duo and our two top editors, after all—but I never asked."

We take our cues from those around us. In an internal interview one security architect would argue that such a document should always be treated as a "five-alarm fire," but it was not treated this way when it was handed to Cole, who carried on treating it with curious nonchalance. It was 2017. "Fake news" was a term that seemed fresh, concerning, as if in using it one was saying something intelligent about the precarious veracity of public information. That some at *The Intercept* immediately declared the document was fake is perhaps unimportant, because any reporter with any classified document would go about authenticating that document. But this thought—that it might be fake—this was another layer of distance between the document and the person behind it. Another reason to lead with curiosity over caution. They considered sending it to Edward Snowden to authenticate, and decided against it.

Cole and Esposito later said, in internal interviews, that they felt rushed. *The Intercept* had recently been scooped by *The Washington Post* on another story; no one wanted that to happen again. It was possible that other reporters at other outlets had the document too.

According to a statement he gave during *The Intercept*'s internal investigation, Cole felt unready to talk to the NSA, but was pressed by Betsy Reed. On Tuesday, May 30, Cole contacted the agency and received a call back from its head of public affairs. Cole described the document; the NSA spokesman asked to see it. Here was something the best digital security team in the business would have certainly advised against, had anyone walked over to their desks. One could argue that Cole would have made that walk had there been an appropriate air of precariousness in the room, had he not been pressed for time, had he had better mentors, had he, like all of us, not found his thoughts flowed so readily to his fingers and his fingers so readily reached for a phone. There is no question that it should have been protocol rather than a decision left for him to make. Cole took pictures of each page of the document with his phone and sent those pictures, using a private PGP key, to the NSA. Whether he spoke with his editors about sending these pictures to the NSA before doing so would, later on, be a matter of contention.

A few days after sending the document to the NSA, Cole, Reed, Esposito, and others gathered in a conference room to talk to the NSA, one of several long meetings in which the NSA may or may not have been stalling. Esposito spoke to a source who said the administration was on a "serious witch hunt" and "going after sources."

On June 5 they were ready to publish, under four bylines, the document and an article explaining its import. There was an air of nervousness in the open office; a couple of staffers, at least, felt it in their stomachs. At the last minute, Betsy Reed asked someone to take a look over the redactions, check that they were solid. He immediately found a small redaction error, which freaked him out, as it was so close to publication. He thought the document should be run through Acrobat Pro to erase watermarks and metadata, but was told there was no time. At 3:44 P.M., *The Intercept* published the piece. They had TV spots scheduled. They were ready for this to be a very big deal. Over five pages, the analysis details "cyber espionage operations" executed by "Russian General Staff Main Intelligence Directorate Actors." There had been, before this leak, sweeping accounts of state-directed Russian interference in the U.S. election. None of them were as detailed as this specific account of a simple phishing operation against an American company, VR Systems, that sells voting-related software.

Later, *The Intercept* would be slammed for publishing a document that showed creases that suggested it was printed, folded, and carried, rather than submitted online, and contained watermarks indicating that it was printed on May 9, 2017, at 6:20 A.M., from a printer with the serial number 535218 or 29535218. The security team at *The Intercept,* the one never consulted, would have known that such a document would only have been accessed under intense surveillance. That a log existed tracking everyone who printed it. The NSA thus knew, from its internal surveillance, that only six people had printed the document. Of those six, only one had emailed *The Intercept* from her work computer, asking for a transcript of a podcast.

Reality had been grocery shopping that Saturday afternoon. She had a date that evening, a first date, with someone she liked but whose own feelings were unclear to her. No one had posted the document; probably, no one ever would. It was an event that had passed through her life. She parked her Cube. Popped the trunk. Filled her arms with groceries. A truck pulled up to the house and three men got out. Her landlord had never taken down the listing for the house—four rooms, $700 a month—and she thought she would have to explain to these people that the place was not, in fact, for rent.

"I'm Justin Garrick," said one of the men, approaching her. "This is my partner, Wally Taylor."

"Hey," said Reality.

"How are you?" asked Wally.

"Good," said Reality. "How you doing?"

"Good," said Justin. "How's your day today?"

"Uh," said Reality. "It's pretty good. Just got some groceries."

"All right," said Justin.

It was hot outside. Reality was making the best money of her life at Pluribus, but she had never been particularly interested in what money can buy. She had rented the place sight unseen, an 800-square-foot house in a part of Augusta the *Atlanta Journal-Constitution* calls "hardscrabble" and her ex-boyfriend calls "blighted"; her neighbors parked their cars on brown, patchy lawns. Reality's grass was newly cut. She hadn't asked anyone to cut it, but she knew who had. There was an old man who went around knocking on doors asking if anyone needed lawn care. When she had been in Belize, the man had cut the grass without her permission. Soon he would come around asking for money.

"Uh, do you know what this might be about?" asked Justin.

"No idea," Reality said.

"This is about, uh, possible mishandling of classified information."

"Oh my goodness."

Reality was still holding the groceries. She had started competitive powerlifting; she was preparing for a competition in three weeks' time. It held off her anxiety. She benched 180. Once, doing box jumps until far beyond the point of exhaustion, she missed the box, fell on her fingers, and shattered numerous bones in her hand. The doctors asked her repeatedly how she could have sustained this kind of injury. Had she been in a fight?

"Would you mind if I at least get some perishables into the fridge?" she asked. Her foster dog, Mickey, a collie mix who had been neglected for years and bred to her own brother, was going wild at the door. In all the years the woman at the dog rescue had been doing her job, only Mickey had bitten her. The woman had called her "a very hard case," hard to place even temporarily, until Reality came along.

"What we are going to have to do is we're going to have to go in the house first to make sure it's safe," said Wally, which is to say, the answer was no. "Is your dog friendly?"

"Okay," said Reality, "she does not like men."

Reality had felt bad boarding Mickey during the trip to

Belize. All the work she had done getting the dog used to the backyard had been undone.

"Okay," said Wally.

"Okay," said Justin. "Do you have a cell phone? We'll take that."

She handed over her iPhone. She'd never set up the security on it; not even a password.

"We're voluntary," said Wally, mysteriously. "Completely up to you. But I think it may be worth your time to listen at least for a little bit."

"Definitely here to comply," said Reality. Later, this would be a point of contention: Was she free to go? Did she know she could just refuse their questions? They were in her house, three men at first, then more. They had her phone.

"Any weapons?"

"I have an AR-15."

"Is it pink?" asked Wally.

"It's pink." Reality laughed nervously. "How did you know? Um, I have a Glock 9 under the bed. And, um, a fifteen-gauge."

"You sound like my house," said Wally.

They walked inside together. Reality leashed up the dog and placed her in the back, where she continued to bark.

"Is that the only pet?" asked Wally.

"There is a cat," said Reality. "She doesn't like men. Starting to see a trend here."

The three of them laughed.

"Come on, girl," said Reality, drawing out the cat from under the couch. "Come here, honey girl."

"Hey sweetie," said Justin to the dog. "Hey sweetie. What's her name?"

"Mickey."

"Hey Mickey."

Reality heard the third man, the one who had never introduced himself, shout in the direction of the street.

"Hey you all, come over here," he said. "Found her like three minutes ago."

The men walked past her, into Reality's TV room. There was an old couch, a TV perched on a trunk with the cord visible. Men walked into her home and took the pictures off the wall—cheaply framed posters: Garth Brooks, the Beatles, Billy Joel, framed pencil sketches of MLK and Gandhi—and checked for anything secreted behind them.

Outside, Justin, Wally, and Reality stood in the driveway. Justin asked her about her foster dog. He had had a foster dog too; the dog would pee when any other man came into the house. As they spoke, Reality heard the sound of furniture being moved.

"He's seven years old now," Justin said. "Just comes up and licks everybody."

"Uh-huh," said Reality.

"Whoever had him before was a real piece of work. Why don't you throw those groceries in the fridge?"

The men found four laptops, a second cell phone. They found her diaries. The rooms were filled with workout equipment, sneakers, and sticky notes on which were scrawled workout regimes ("Bench 5X5, Back Squat 5X5") but also stray thoughts about issues with which she was preoccupied ("Peace-making is less of a rational-economic model of dividing resources and territory fairly," "Further research: Deserts versus rainforest").

Reality was granted permission to walk into her own house by the men who had shown up there unannounced. She placed the bags on the counter as a man took a Pokémon blanket off her bed. Reality's back was to the men. Under their watch, she slowly lifted popsicles out of a paper bag and placed them in the freezer.

"House is cleared," said the third man. Reality closed the freezer and returned outside.

"Do you have a place in the house that we can kind of sit that's away?" said Justin.

"Away? Hm. I don't like to go in there," she said, gesturing toward the back room.

"You don't like to go in there."

"Oh gosh, it's just creepy. It's always dirty and—"

"Okay," said Justin.

Every motion she made in the house was now under their watch. There was the possibility that she would tamper with her things, which were now only her things for so long as the FBI agents decided to let her keep them. The door was open.

"Can I close the door for my cat?" she asked.

Wally held out her phone. "How do we open this?"

"Press that. There you go."

The men in her house were now taking pictures. Outside, there was no shade. Justin swatted at a gnat on his neck. He had a sinus infection; his voice was gravelly, and the heat was hard to take.

Reality's dog howled and growled and barked at the agents. Justin started talking about his rescue dog again. It once chewed through three Apple power cords.

"Ninety bucks a pop," he said.

"Yep," said Reality.

It was weird to be separated from her phone. How long was all of this going to last? "I didn't want to make any assumptions or anything like that," she said, looking at

Wally messing with her phone, “but I am teaching yoga tomorrow and my phone has music on it.”

“Okay,” said Justin.

“Um, I could make do,” said Reality. She didn’t want to antagonize them, seem uncooperative. They were FBI agents and she was former air force. They all understood hierarchy, cooperation. “Like, there are bigger problems in the world, I guess,” she said.

They walked into the creepy back room, which had always given her a bad feeling, as if she had intuited what was to come. There was only a kennel she never used. The baseboards were lined with grime, and the blinds were all broken; her fat cat loved to claw at them.

“Do you have a few chairs, like a kitchen table and chairs we can pull into that back room?” asked Justin.

“No,” said Reality, laughing. She had not wanted to consider Augusta permanent. The house was a barely furnished rental with a couch, a TV, a bed, and three guns. She was looking for jobs abroad. Why invest in a table?

“This room is dirty,” said Reality. “I’m so sorry.”

“You live here by yourself?” asked Justin.

“Yes.”

“Very hard without a table and chairs,” he said. They laughed quietly.

“I’m so sorry.”

“It’s—you don’t have to apologize. It’s your house. Um, if you—if you do feel like, you know, you want to sit or anything like that, we’ll sit, okay? You know, we can sit on the floor, I don’t care. If you sit on the floor, I’ll sit on the floor.”

Reality sat on the floor. Justin and Wally stayed beside her, and showed her the warrant that authorized them to search her home, her car, her phone, and her body. She skimmed it.

"A hundred and forty-five pounds," she said. "You guys flatter me."

"It was on your driver's license."

"I lied."

"Um," said Justin, "all this stems from a report that we received that you had mishandled classified information, okay? So, that's, uh, the broad scope of it. Does that—does that ring any bells to you whatsoever?"

"It does now," said Reality. She shifted her weight. Justin's back was against a dirty wall, looking out into the yard, where the dog had finally given up.

"Do you know about PKI passwords?" she asked.

"Uh-huh," said Justin.

On her second day at Pluribus, she told the agents, she had not been assigned a desk. She had printed out an email containing passwords she needed to do her job. She had placed everything in a folder, passed through security to the Whitelaw cafeteria, and gone to a Starbucks. When she came back through security, guards found the classified document. They wrote up a report.

"But you were still in the building?" asked Justin.

"Yeah."

"Okay. All right. So as far as you're aware, you haven't committed any security violations or anything you're aware of, other than—than this PKI thing?"

"Other than the PKI thing, no. I do print documents at work," said Reality, "because it's just easier for me to translate them by hand."

"Got it," said Justin.

"After that stupid PKI thing," said Reality, "I was like, no more white paper out of the building." Asked about a violation, Reality's mind had jumped to printouts.

"So you said you printed out stuff?" asked Justin.

"Yeah," said Reality.

"Is there a—why did that come to mind as far as security?" asked Justin.

"Um, it just. I guess it always, I just think about um, you know, having actual papers. I can't imagine any other way to get things out of the building, I guess. I'm old-fashioned, so I'm just thinking about that."

"Nothing got out of the building?"

"Nothing."

"You didn't carry anything out of the building?"

"No. No."

"Have you ever inadvertently gone outside your access of need-to-know items?"

Sometimes, Reality slipped back into her old life, watching video of her friends dropping missiles from drones. She had access to the video feed of the destruction, and the chats as it went down. Sometimes, she printed out documents that interested her that did not particularly relate to Iranian aerospace, which bored her. At the top right of her screen at work there was a box that said TOP ARTICLE. There had been one about miniature ponies. Had they heard about that?

"I missed that one," said Justin. Wally laughed.

"Okay," said Justin. "Um, you've kind of already answered this: Have you ever taken anything out of, uh, the NSA facility?"

"No."

"No? Okay. Hm."

"How's the neighborhood?" asked Wally.

"I did not look at a map when I signed the lease," said Reality, "but I'm well armed."

"You seem to be."

"Okay. Reality, what if I said that I have the information to suggest you did print out something outside the scope of your work?"

"Okay. I would have to try to remember."

"Reality," said Wally, gently, "we obviously know a lot more than what we're telling you at this point. And I think you know a lot more than what you're telling us at this point. I don't want you to go down the wrong road. I think you need to stop and think about what you're saying and what you're doing. I think there's an opportunity to maybe tell the truth. Because telling a lie to an FBI agent is not going to be the right thing."

"Mm-hmm," said Reality.

"Okay? Um, you know, and again," said Wally, "we're here voluntarily. You're talking voluntarily. I'm not asking you—forcing you to do anything."

"There was one I printed out because I wanted to read it," said Reality. "It looked like a piece of history. I read it and I burn-bagged it. It was early April, late March."

"Okay," said Justin. "How about any other times?"

"I just kept tabs on those articles. Just kept reading them."

"Okay. Did you ever go searching for them? Ever go digging?"

"Nothing more than a ten-minute distraction from work."

"What was the timing around it?"

"I'm trying to— I remember that week, I got in a fight with the boyfriend that week. Um, April. Let's see, March, April. When did I break up with him?" She sighed. "Maybe we started dating in March, so . . . it had to have been sometime in April. Um. I'm just really going blank on what week that was. I'm trying to think what weekend—what the weekend was like after that. I'm so sorry."

"Okay. All right. What if l told you that I know that you searched for and printed out a document on the ninth of May?"

"Uh, I guess I—I can't argue that. If you—obviously you know."

"Yeah."

"It's been a really bad month for me, so."

"Okay," said Justin wearily. "What did you do with that document?"

"Like I said, I kept it on my desk for three days because I thought it was interesting and I thought I would read it. And then I put it in the burn bag."

"You put it in the burn bag?"

"Yeah."

"Reality, are you sure that's what you did with it?"

"Yes."

"You're positive?"

"Yes."

"You didn't take it out of the building?"

"No."

"You didn't send it?"

"No."

"You didn't send it to anyone?"

"No."

Wally sighed again.

"Reality, can you guess how many people printed the document? Not many. The document has made it outside. Obviously. Because we are here."

"Obviously."

"The most likely candidate, far and away, is you. Now, I don't think you're a big bad master spy, okay? I don't think that. I've looked at the evidence and it's compelling. Now, I'm not sure why you did it, and I'm curious as to that, but I think you might've been angry over everything that's going on, politics-wise. Because you can't turn on the—you can't turn on the TV without getting pissed off. Or at least I can't. And I think you might have made a mistake. So I ask again, did you take it out and send it?"

"I didn't. I put it in the burn bag."

Justin sighed.

"I mean, I'm trying to deploy. I'm not trying to be a whistleblower. That's crazy."

"So how do you think the document made it out?"

"I mean, let's be serious," said Reality. "There's no security on documents."

"What if I told you that document made its way to an outlet you subscribe to. See, things are starting to get a little specific. Which is very, very, very compelling. I'd like to know the reason, because I don't think you make a habit out of this at all. At all. Would you agree this looks awfully bad?"

"It looks really bad."

The agents paused. They sensed a new openness, born of exhaustion.

"If you're angry about what's going on," said Justin, "if there's something that . . . Look, you've had a good career. You have. If there's something that just pushed you over the edge on this, now is the perfect time. This is a podium."

Reality's mother and sister had always maintained that we live in a just country, bound by rules. In the end, intentions matter. Truth matters. Good people will be revealed as such.

"Maybe you made a mistake," said Wally. "Maybe you weren't thinking for a minute. Maybe you got angry, like he said. If that's the case, then that makes us feel a little better, knowing that we don't have a—a real serious problem here. You know, uh—uh, that's something that concerns us, too, this isn't an ongoing problem. But we need to figure it out. And if it was a mistake, let's deal with it."

A good system would recognize the good. A good system might even be able, once this was all sorted out, to let her walk. She was not a dangerous person. There was no malice in the act. *Mistake* was the word he used.

The men were still searching the house, their boots on Afghan rugs she'd bought from a dealer in Maryland. He was so surprised the first time she walked in and starting speaking Pashto. After that first time, she visited frequently, just to practice.

"So how did you get it out of the building?" asked Justin.

"Folded in half in my pantyhose."

There was such relief in saying it, the encounter no longer adversarial.

"It's just been hard at work because—I've filed formal complaints about them having Fox News on, you know? Uh, just at least for God's sake put Al Jazeera on, or a slideshow of people's pets. I've tried everything to get that changed."

"I think pets might be the way to go," laughed Justin.

The men became even more solicitous. Did she want some water? Tap or filtered? The third man was still trying to get the cat out from under the bed. "I don't think you'll fit in there anymore," he said. "She's a big girl."

"Yeah, we're trying," said Reality. "She's on my lease as Queen Latifah. But we're trying to get her down to like a Beyoncé size ten? Girl likes to eat."

"When she came out I was like whoa," said the third man.

Five years previous to this, Reality and her family had walked out of a restaurant and noticed a tiny black kitten with its eyes closed. Brittany insisted on taking it home, and then to the vet. The vet told them he had an infection and needed to be put down. Brittany pressed; wasn't there anything they could do to save him? The vet said both of the kitten's eyes could be removed. Brittany told him to do it. Now she had a spirited blind cat she frequently referred to as her "firstborn son."

Justin brought Reality water. He asked what else they would find. Reality told them about her Tor Browser. About a time when she'd opened WikiLeaks, just to see what was there. She told them about the time when she had stuck a thumb drive into a secret computer at Fort Meade, to see how it was that her colleagues were loading pictures onto the "high side," which is what one calls the closed network of computers at the NSA.

"Have you had any contact with anyone else?" asked Justin.

"No. It's like you said, I just saw the article and was like, I don't understand why this isn't a thing. And it— I just—"

"It made you very mad," said Wally.

"It made me very mad," said Reality.

"I— I just— I guess I didn't care about, like, myself at that point, and just . . . Yeah. I guess. Yeah, I screwed up royally."

"Okay. Is there anything else that you want to tell me about? Say? Talk about why?"

Reality Winner was a twenty-five-year-old in quarter-life crisis who was not allowed to talk about the source of that crisis. Her last relationship had just ended; her father was dead. She was not allowed to complain to her mother about the stress of translating words that resulted in corpses; not allowed to talk about incompetent coworkers, or the futility of her work, about the status differences between contractors like herself and NSA employees. She couldn't tell other people about the fact that they played Fox News in the room, and that on Fox News she watched people debating the existence of facts to which she had special access. But these men already knew about her life, the world of classification, the high side and PKI passwords, sources and methods. She could tell them. And wouldn't they understand better than most? They too had to keep secrets from their families. They understood, they said, that in a moment of anger she had made a mistake.

"No, it was just . . ." said Reality. "Yeah, just that, that day, that week, it was just too much to just sit back and watch it and think, why do I have this job if I'm just going to sit back and be helpful and you know just—it was just . . . I thought that was the final straw. I had, you know, seven, eight months left of a job that didn't mean anything to me. I felt really hopeless and, um, seeing that information that had been contested back and forth and back and forth in the public domain for so long, like, with everything else that keeps getting released and keeps getting leaked, why isn't this out there?"

"Do you have any questions for me?" asked Justin.

"So many," said Reality. "Um. This sounds really bad. Am I going to jail tonight?"

"I don't know the answer to that," said Justin.

Reality was worried about the animals. Someone would have to call Cathy at the Humane Society.

"We're not going to leave the animals," said Wally, "I promise you."

"Is there anything at the—at your desk at work that I should be worried about?" asked Justin.

"I have an Anderson Cooper photo that is signed," said Reality. "It's not legit."

The men laughed.

"He's quite good-looking," said Reality, "so that is something that you must contend with."

"The man cuts a figure," said Justin, "what can you say?"

The men searching her house were about to enter the bathroom. Did she have any weapons in there? There were nail clippers in her makeup bag, she said. She waited while they searched the last of the rooms.

When the girls were in trouble, it was their stepfather they called. Mom would panic, but Gary would fix it. Billie and Gary were at home in Texas, getting dressed for what they called "dinner and dominoes," pizza followed by game night in the neighbors' dining room. Billie was deciding what to wear when she heard Gary on the phone. "I love you," he said. "Are you okay?" She didn't know who he was talking to.

"I'm in trouble," Reality said. "I'm probably going to be arrested and detained." She handed her phone back to Wallace. The details, he said, were classified.

Billie had no idea what they were supposed to do, knowing their daughter had been arrested, but Gary reasoned that it wouldn't make anything better to sit in their living room, worrying. "Let's just hold off," he said, "and see what we learn."

They proceeded to their neighbors' house and played a game of dominoes, which is what they were doing when Reality called back. She needed her parents to come to Georgia. Knowing only that there would be a court appearance of some kind, they packed up the car and left South Texas for Augusta at 7:00 the next morning. They drove twenty-one hours, straight through the night, listening to a book on tape. Driving out of Texas, they passed a dead alligator on the side of the road.

No one had yet told Reality that she was going to be arrested. What the men said was that they needed to pat her down, but they had failed to bring a woman officer, and so they had to call for one. It had already been hours; Reality waited some more. *What happened to Chelsea Manning?* she asked herself. *She was disappeared to Quantico.* Quantico was a seven-hour drive. Is that where they were going? Reality realized she didn't actually know much about Snowden or Manning; every time she searched, it felt criminal, and so she had never gone deep. She wondered now what law it was, exactly, they had broken. It had never occurred to her, before today, that she might be breaking the same one. She had thought of it as a workplace infraction.

The FBI agents left her with women officers from the sheriff's office. The next time she saw Wally and Justin they'd be in a courtroom, testifying against her. The women did not take Reality to Quantico, but to the Lincoln County Jail, where a gentle guard told her to take off her clothes, handed her a jumpsuit, and took her picture. Reality looked at the picture of herself on the guard's camera. Her hair was greasy; she thought she looked fat. "Can you put an Instagram filter on it?" she asked.

For all that *The Intercept* had given the NSA—advance

notice, multiple opportunities for redaction, even, incredibly, the document itself—the NSA withheld key information from the publication. Two days after Cole sent the document, and two days before *The Intercept* published the story, the source was already in jail.

THE TIME FOR PARDONS

I have never felt safer than I felt as a twenty-one-year-old in Myanmar. I mean this sincerely, well aware of the privilege it entails. As a person not particularly subject to tyranny in a tyrannical state, I was a potential problem. Thus, I was always watched. I could walk streets alone, late at night, and never worry; I feared for the lives of many people, but questions of my own safety literally never came to mind. I remember distinctly coming back to D.C., twenty-two years old, walking down Sixteenth Street at 4:00 A.M., and as a car slowed and a man stared, realizing that the protective gaze was gone.

The gaze of the state was a comfort because the consequences appeared clear and unthreatening; if I crossed a boundary, I would simply be put on a plane and sent home. I would not feel a moment's fear in Myanmar, until years later, when I flew back to Yangon, and as I made my way through passport control a half dozen airport personnel pulled me away and encircled me and shouted at one another in words I could not make out, and suddenly I did not understand the rules. I had published something critical of the government in a Saturday edition of the *Los Angeles Times,* I recalled as

I waited for whatever was coming my way, but I wasn't sure anyone read the Saturday edition of the *Los Angeles Times,* least of all the Myanmar junta. In later years the young publisher of our newspaper would be locked up for a full eight years under charges related to censorship, and a journalist from Michigan would be sent to Myanmar's Insein prison under false pretenses. My sense of security all those years ago had never been warranted, the rules had never been clear, though I am glad to have been unaware of dangers that did not materialize. I was put on a golf cart and driven to a nearly full plane that had evidently not been allowed to leave until I was definitively denied entrance.

In 2008, while Joseph Biggs was still in Afghanistan, a reporter from *GQ* had embedded with his unit. Michael Hastings wrote about whistleblowers and deep-state operatives; his reporting would later lead to the resignation of General Stanley McChrystal from his post as commander in Afghanistan. Biggs, he of the "hard dick" who wanted to "fucking fight," was skeptical of soft reporters, but Hastings appeared to be fearless, and the two became friends. Five years later, when Biggs was unemployed back in the States, Hastings wrote an email to his colleagues at *BuzzFeed,* and also to Biggs, that read, "The Feds are interviewing my 'close friends and associates.'" He was "onto a big story." He would go "off the rada[r] for a bit." On the next day, speeding in a Mercedes through Hollywood, the car hit a palm tree and burst into flames. Hastings was dead.

Biggs did not think it was an accident. He had screamed in the night beating back memories of a war he thought to be sold on lies, and here he saw, again, the secret workings of the deep state. He contacted reporters about the email.

"He said what a lot of people were scared to say," Biggs told the local news.

When Alex Jones called him, Joe Biggs was on his way to a UFC fight in Myrtle Beach. Biggs had recently spent years abroad; he was not, as they say, "extremely online," and he had never heard of Jones, the country's most powerful conspiracy theorist, so he could not know, in that moment, that he had found his vocation.

Biggs went on Infowars to talk about Hastings. He came back to talk about Hastings many times. The conversations would wander to war stories. Biggs said he was told to go to Afghanistan to "win hearts and minds" but the memories he related were of the DEA torturing Afghan farmers. Jones offered Biggs a job at Infowars. The job title was "investigative journalist." Biggs did not have to learn, as Assange had, that to make people listen you had to put on a show, as spectacle-making comprised his entire journalistic education. The conspiracy Biggs was best known for promoting was about a human trafficking ring said to be headquartered in a D.C. pizza place. He stopped trying to kill himself. He was recognized at the airport. Sometimes he saw people slinking away from him, having taken a picture.

When Kiriakou was released in 2015 he was a felon, and as a felon he applied to any job of which he could think: Target, McDonald's, Starbucks. "Nothing," he says. "No response."

His attention thus turned to a presidential pardon, which he believed he might be able to secure as a former CIA official who had gone on the record about torture. In 2015, when Hillary Clinton was expected to succeed Obama, the politics of a pardon seemed hopeless. By 2016 the politics of a pardon had been rendered promisingly bizarre.

"WikiLeaks," said Trump on the trail in 2016, "I love

WikiLeaks," and "It's been amazing what's coming out on WikiLeaks," and "This WikiLeaks is like a treasure trove." By the time Reality leaked the document, a realignment had taken place. No one was claiming that WikiLeaks was a "media darling"; the question was, rather, whether WikiLeaks, in its intention to help Donald Trump win an election, had successfully contributed to the win.

In 2011 dictator Muammar al-Qaddafi is being beaten to death by his former subjects. He's just been pulled from a drainage pipe in which he was hiding. Someone is filming. Half Qaddafi's face and head are soaked in blood, down to the ends of his black hair. He tries to wipe the blood from his face, but there is already blood on his hand, and far too much on his face to wipe away, and for a moment, the man, moments from death, stares in wonder at his fingers. Five thousand miles from Libya, someone tells Hillary Clinton that the military operation she convinced a reluctant Obama to approve has been successful. The armed Predator drones sent in to track and fire had set off a chain of events that ended in Qaddafi's death. "We came, we saw, he died!" laughs Clinton, on camera.

It is now well established that the murder of this particular Middle Eastern strongman led, just as it had in Iraq, to a disastrous power vacuum. There was no plan to contain the weapons left behind by Qaddafi, including missiles that could take down a plane; for Americans to buy them would create incentive for Libyans to import even more weapons. Surface-to-air missiles, the U.S. defense secretary later said, "basically just disappeared into the maw of the Middle East and North Africa." It was a regional arms free-for-all unlike anything since Vietnam. Qatar and the UAE began arming rebel factions. Libya had become a source of weapons for Tunisia, Somalia, Egypt. In 2014, ISIS arrived, and began taking territory. Off the coast inflatable floats packed with migrants left for Europe; sometimes they were turned away, and sometimes the boats shipwrecked, and sometimes the bodies of drowned children washed ashore. A baby blanket, but no baby, appeared on a beach in Tripoli. Europe stopped exporting inflatable boats to Libya. Clinton, in failing to learn the lessons of Iraq—another intervention of which she had been supportive—had helped to create a failed state. Obama admitted that it should have been handled differently. It was, to Assange, precisely the kind of moralizing imperialist arrogance he wanted to expose. The careless violence of it.

"A vote today for Hillary Clinton is a vote for endless, stupid war," Assange wrote shortly after Clinton narrowly won the Iowa caucus, from his 330 feet of space in the Ecuadorean embassy. "Hillary didn't just vote for Iraq. She made her own Iraq. Libya is Hillary's Iraq and if she becomes president she will make more. I have had years of experience in dealing with Hillary Clinton and have read thousands of her cables. Hillary lacks judgement and will push the United States into endless, stupid wars which spread terrorism.... She's a war hawk with bad judgement who gets an unseemly emotional rush out of killing people." He posted the video of Clinton laughing. *We came, we saw, he died.*

Having to choose between Clinton and Trump in 2016, Assange said, was like having to choose between "cholera and gonorrhea," but he did not seem to find that choice very hard; there was the devil he knew and the devil who at least pretended not to have supported the war in Iraq. "We believe it would be much better for GOP to win," Assange told a private group via DM. Clinton, he said, was "a bright, well connected, sadistic sociopath." A former WikiLeaks volunteer sent the conversation to the press. Fans of WikiLeaks would have liked to believe that the platform was neutral, but Assange made it hard to argue that it was so.

Clinton's campaign chairman received an email in March 2016. "Hi John," the email read. "Someone just used your password to try to sign into your Google Account. You should change your password immediately." There was a link. Podesta's chief of staff forwarded it to a computer technician. The technician wrote back: "This is a legitimate email." He now says he meant to say, *This is not a legitimate email.* Someone clicked, and in doing so, granted hackers access to tens of thousands of private emails. It was a simple phishing attack, not unlike the one described in the document Reality leaked.

The hackers sent the emails to Assange, who claimed no knowledge of or responsibility for their origin. He published the emails from Hillary's campaign not as a dump but as a monthslong tease, a devastating series of emails from the embassy in which he had promised not to interfere in world affairs. "You need both a public and a private position," Clinton had told some lobbyists, which is precisely what Assange maintained about feminism.

It was a "close reading" of these emails, a creative take on their "hidden messages," that led to Pizzagate, the conspiracy Joe Biggs is best known for promoting. In the summer, just before the Democratic convention, WikiLeaks published 20,000 emails about Clinton, some of which showed the DNC pushing for Hillary over Bernie. There was for instance an email suggesting the DNC go hard against Bernie Sanders's faith. ("Does he believe in a God," asked a party official. "This could make several points difference with . . . my peeps.") Fans of the DNC would have liked to believe the party was neutral, but the emails made that difficult.

The Democrats' response was to drive attention away from the embarrassing content of the emails, which hurt the candidate they'd been revealed to prefer, to the motivation for the leak. "Experts are telling us that Russian state actors broke into the DNC, took all these emails and now are leaking them out through these websites," a Clinton campaign manager told George Stephanopoulos. It was an act of espionage, they said, aided and abetted by WikiLeaks. In the summer of 2016, this sounded, to pretty much everyone, like paranoid spy-movie talk. It sounded especially so to the most prominent voices at *The Intercept,* for whom unsubstantiated accusations of Russian election interference recalled the baseless assumptions on which the Iraq War had been launched.

"Any of us who grew up in politics or came of age as an American in the '60s or '70s or the '80s knows that central to American political discourse has always been trying to tie your political opponents to Russia," Glenn Greenwald said on *Democracy Now*. "And it's amazing to have watched, in this campaign, Democrats completely resurrect that Cold War McCarthyite kind of rhetoric." There was a kind of contingent digging in, an arbitrary selection of sides, in a realm where facticity and contrarianism sometimes intersected and sometimes did not. The intelligence community had aligned on a narrative that tied Russia to election interference and the intelligence community had lied about mass surveillance, had constructed the false pretense that led to war with Iraq, had operated, for a long time now, well outside of democratic accountability. At 10:49 A.M. on July 27, 2016, speaking to press, candidate Trump claimed to be a fan of torture and also invited Russia to hack further into Hillary Clinton's emails. "I will tell you this: Russia, if you're listening, I hope you're able to find the thirty thousand emails that are missing." It sounded like a joke, and well might have been, though by that evening, Russian hackers had begun to try to break into the servers used by Clinton's personal office.

The speech President Donald Trump gave to members of the Central Intelligence Agency on January 21, 2017, was a variation on his usual standup routine, the winkingly self-aggrandizing cad, the Freewheeling Narcissist, in on the joke. He seemed a little bored with the character this time, a little tired of his own shtick. Everyone in the room, he said, had probably voted for him. He bragged about his intellect ("trust me, I'm like a smart person") and his stamina and the size of his inaugural crowd ("looked like a million, a million and a half"). There was the stilted attempt at generosity ("this group is going to be one of the most important groups in the country") and there were the usual attacks on the media ("they showed a field where there was practically nobody standing there"), at which point the character broke down a little, because the inaugural crowd thing clearly bothered him in a way it wouldn't have bothered the Freewheeling Narcissist. He said he had been on the cover of *Time* "fourteen or fifteen times, the all-time record in the history of *Time* magazine," which it wasn't. "I love honesty," he said.

It was not a notable speech but for where it was given, which was in the lobby at Langley, in front of a marble wall in which were etched 128 stars. Each of the stars represents an agent killed while on assignment. Some have names but many do not; their identities and missions remain secret, in service of the kind of propaganda meant to provide the agency with a sense of itself, sacred and self-important. Former CIA director John Brennan called Trump's performance "a despicable display of self-aggrandizement" and said Trump should be "ashamed of himself."

This public display of disrespect, this simple unwillingness to provide easy platitudes in a realm where they had always been offered, was a low point for an intelligence community that had recently been credited with billions of dollars, trusted to spend those billions well and without oversight, assumed to be safekeeping the security of a nation though they wouldn't or couldn't tell anyone precisely how. Over time they had built a secret parallel infrastructure that sucked data from cell phones and laptops and processed that data in anonymous buildings across the country, from Tampa to Salt Lake to Indianapolis. They had hired tens of thousands of ordinary Americans in ordinary places and forbidden them from talking about their jobs with their ordinary friends and family. They had murdered hundreds of people with flying robots and tortured dozens of innocent people in countries where this was less trouble than it would have been stateside. They had spied on Americans without a warrant and punished their own when they tried to point this out. The intelligence community was, for a long and expensive period, identified with seriousness itself, and it continued to be so for most people through 2013, when Edward Snowden released thousands of documents revealing unsavory and illegal activities.

And for a long while it seemed that this would be the threat to their legitimacy: insistent, monotone, analytical men on the Far Left and libertarian Right most comfortable debating, in exhaustive detail, the history of the Fourth Amendment. But that was not the real threat. Because Donald Trump was the furthest thing from Far Left or libertarian Right, and as he came to power, two things became clear: he was a savant at undermining legitimacy, and he considered the intelligence community an enemy whose legitimacy needed to be undermined. Instead of objecting to their individual crimes, he drew attention to the whole structure—a secret, parallel government of officials running secret programs with secret money. Trump supporters could not know what went on at Langley or Fort Meade and so Donald Trump painted a picture for them: a bunch of men no one had elected, whose names no one knows, conspiring to destroy the man they had chosen to lead them. He saw a solid foundation and on it built an imaginary world. This was the deep state.

Trump had absolutely no impulse to transparency. There was nothing in him that desired to limit executive power. His attitude toward power was straightforwardly authoritarian, constrained primarily by incompetence. On torture, Trump said he would "bring back a hell of a lot worse than waterboarding." On Guantánamo Bay: "We're going to load it up with some bad dudes." Leakers, he said, were "traitors and cowards." Snowden "should be executed." He was a simple, phenomenally successful program that operated by personal vendetta. His principle strategy was eroding trust in established authority.

In January, the intelligence community, including the FBI and CIA and NSA, released a report stating that Putin himself had ordered the hack on the DNC, that Russia had engaged in a campaign to help Trump, and that Putin wanted to discredit both Clinton and the American electoral system itself.

The word for what Trump was doing to the deep state was *troll*. He habitually divulged classified information. He fired people in key positions and either did not replace them or replaced them with men who knew little about those institutions. "Your inflammatory rhetoric, insults, lies, & encouragement of physical violence are disgraceful," John Brennan told Trump on Twitter. "When the full extent of your venality, moral turpitude, and political corruption becomes known, you will take your rightful place as a disgraced demagogue in the dustbin of history." In Helsinki, Trump met with Putin behind closed doors. Asked by the press whether Trump believed that Putin had interfered in the election, he said, "President Putin, he just said it's not Russia. I don't see any reason why it would be." To which @JohnBrennan tweeted: "Donald Trump's press conference performance in Helsinki rises to & exceeds the threshold of 'high crimes & misdemeanors.' It was nothing short of treasonous."

James Clapper, who had not long ago lied to Congress about the NSA's activities and then been exposed by Snowden, mused on national television that Trump might be a Russian asset. He was agreeing with a former deputy director of the FBI. Russia's state-controlled television network ran a segment called "Clinton and ISIS Funded by the Same Money" featuring Julian Assange. The FBI and CIA and NSA were, in Trump's view, attacking his legitimacy, employing his favored tactic against him. He would therefore spend his presidency attacking their legitimacy, alongside that of the U.S. electoral system.

When Trump talked about the vast, unaccountable

secret state built by his predecessors, he sounded like an intern at *The Intercept.* "Unelected deep state operatives who defy the voters to push their own secret agendas are truly a threat to democracy itself," he told supporters at a rally—there were presidential rallies now—in Montana.

Americans on the left and right are equally likely to believe that the government is secretly surveilling them; the belief that the government is unaccountable is not meaningfully partisan. It was not so hard, then, to convince many people already inclined to believe Trump that a vast state was lining up to defy them and undermine him. The way this deep state would do so, according to this school of thought, would be to frame him for colluding with Russia to interfere in the election.

In 2016, when Reality Winner came upon evidence of a single, specific attack on the voting system, mainstream liberals insisted that all the evidence pointed to Trump being a stooge of Putin. The Right and the libertarian Left claimed this was a story useful to the deep state, short on evidence, propagated by a willing media.

Trump was elected at a time when Reality Winner was trying and failing to find a position that would take her to Afghanistan, where she could talk rather than merely listen. He assumed office days before she gave up and accepted the work for which the United States had trained her. She was not then thinking about Russia. Her work was with Iran. Her heart with Afghanistan.

That Glenn Greenwald had become the Left's most vociferous skeptic of Russian election interference, increasingly closed off from evidence, remained, through this period, inside baseball. That he was sliding into position as a right-wing media star was the kind of thing you knew if it was your job to know it. If you were a twenty-five-year-old worried about the world, you likely thought of *The Intercept* as the publication of Snowden and Manning, a friend to Assange, an antagonistic publication that refused to take the administration's talking points. Reality turned to *The Intercept* for news of Chelsea Manning and the war in Yemen; she had once emailed the publication asking for a transcript of a podcast about climate change. She did not turn to it for news of collusion between Russia and Trump, a narrative of which its most recognizable personalities were deeply skeptical.

This was also an attitude shared by conservative media supportive of Trump, which now required a very specific sort of talking head. Someone from the deep state who held no loyalty toward it. Someone who could catalog its crimes in the service of legitimizing attacks on the president.

On the day Tucker Carlson's producers called, John Kiriakou practiced answers in his head for hours. He knew exactly what he would say, who the audience was. They sent him the questions ahead of time—softballs "as big as beach balls as they're coming in" he told me, but he didn't need to look very closely. He knew what Fox wanted, and he intended to deliver it.

"You worked for CIA for a long time under John Brennan who ultimately backed your prosecution for a crime I don't think would be considered a crime today," said Tucker Carlson. Between them was a collage of a donkey, a Russian cathedral, and Robert Mueller under the words THE COLLUSION HOAX.

"So tell me your perspective on Robert Mueller being trotted out as an expert on Russia."

"An expert," said Kiriakou, slowly, with a performance

of great disappointment. "I think this was scandalous, for a number of reasons, the most important of which is that John Brennan has repeatedly used the word 'treason,' the word 'traitor,' when describing the president. Treason is a death penalty charge!" He looked credibly scandalized. "Is he seriously saying the president ought to be . . . executed? To me John Brennan is simply not a serious person. He shouldn't be taken seriously by us. Or by anybody else. I worked with John Brennan over many, many years. I always thought that he was in over his head intellectually, and I think he's proven that repeatedly."

"It's funny you should say that," said Tucker. "I think the default assumption for people including me is that the director of the CIA is a very smart man. I've watched him closely and I've concluded that he's not very bright. I'm not attacking him! It's okay," said Tucker. Tucker tried to look a little sad about it.

"No, no!" Kiriakou assured him. "It's an observation!"

"But it's clearly the case. How does a guy like that run the CIA?" asked Tucker. The two men discussed it for a while and came to a conclusion: "pure cronyism."

"The results of all of this stuff," Tucker said, "is that the ordinary person—me, everyone else—knows that these agencies are run by people much less impressive than we thought, with political agendas, and in some cases ruthless and cruel. You're one of the people who felt the sting of that—you went to prison."

"I did, thanks to John Brennan."

"Where are the pardons here?" asked Tucker. "Is it time for the executive branch to send a really clear message we are going to stop the destruction of innocent people by out-of-control bureaucrats?"

John's eyes were wide. He had never been more ready. "I think it is the time for pardons," he said. "The American people understand that people have been wronged. . . . it's time to wipe the slate."

"It doesn't make sense not to pardon people!" said Tucker.

"I agree! Wipe the slate clean."

IT COULD BE YOUR SISTER

On June 3, 2017, Brittany Winner was celebrating a fifth wedding anniversary with her husband, Chris, a fellow scientist, at a showing of *Wonder Woman*. She was thrilled by it, though her phone buzzed a dozen times during the film from a strange number she assumed to be persistent spam. Later, the number appeared eight more times. (*If you get a spam phone call,* Brittany would joke later, *pick it up. It could be your sister who needs you who is in jail.*) When Billie finally called Brittany and told her Reality was locked up, Brittany assumed it was a bar fight. Someone had triggered her little sister's temper.

"Oh Britty," Reality said, when Brittany finally answered, back in her Maryland apartment. "I screwed up."

"Well it's gonna be okay."

Brittany was eighty-three days from defending her dissertation in pharmacology and toxicology. Her sister had a history of intruding.

"I don't know if I'm getting out of this one . . ."

"You survived basic training."

"Basic training is like college," said Reality. "You're getting ready for something. This, I mean, and the food, and I don't, I can't even get over the little things, like I was supposed to teach yoga today, I was supposed to be on a date last night. I have a powerlifting competition at the end of the night. I know it's stupid, but that's my whole life, that's all I had."

"It's not stupid," said Brittany. "In fact Chris is worried about you. Chris was like what's she gonna eat. I was like the only thing she eats is kale so . . ."

"I know, I feel absolutely terrible, there's so much white bread here, I . . . I—"

"I'm sorry I'm laughing at you," said Brittany, laughing.

They joked about *Orange Is the New Black,* and Reality, embarrassed but unable to shake the worry of obligation, asked her sister to arrange for a substitute for a cycling class on Wednesday and for her name to be removed from the roster on Saturday. She had already arranged for the care of Mickey, her dog, and Mina, the cat; that was the first call she made.

"I finally found someone," she sighed. Reality often felt guilty when she wasn't working out, which was a hindrance to her dating and social lives. She could not relax and drink a beer because it was not relaxing to be taking in calories without burning them, to be wasting away when you could be powerlifting. But now there was this guy she could work out with for hours, a way to connect with another person and feel at peace. Reality wasn't yet sure what his feelings were, and she had just missed their first date.

"I feel like I'm being a diva," said Reality, "like there are freakin' Syrian refugees that have nothing but still go from one day to the next. I just don't want to spend years in prison."

"I think it's still going to be okay," said Brittany.

"I didn't think. I did not think of the consequences for even a second. It was a stupid decision."

"Well everyone makes stupid decisions. You're going to get through this."

"I keep telling myself to act more like I did something wrong," said Reality, and laughed.

"What?"

"That was the thing when the FBI was interrogating me, they were just like, look we just want to know why. You know what I mean? They were just straight-up curious to know why."

"Well, maybe you're right," said Brittany. "I don't mean to discount the effect of being pretty and white and blond. I'm kidding."

"I'm definitely playing that card. I'm going to braid my hair, I'm going to look cute like . . ."

Brittany was laughing.

"I'm going to have a small voice, I'm going to, you know—"

"Cry a lot."

In 2017 Titus Nichols is a thirty-six-year-old Black lawyer in the Southern District of Georgia. He has represented clients accused of murder and burglary and bank robbery, and he is a practical person. He is not romantic about the law. "I am not someone," he says, "who thinks, *Oh!* The jury is gonna rise up and do the right thing." When he goes to the federal courthouse in Augusta, he passes by a display of lovingly preserved letters from Georgians writing to say they would not be present for jury duty, as they were busy fighting for the Confederacy.

The Southern District of Georgia likes to keep things lean.

It does not have its own prison, and it does not have a public defender's office; it merely has a list of attorneys who will consider taking on indigent offenders for the small amount of pay the state will proffer. Nichols had put himself on the list as a way to get trial experience. He had been a JAG officer, and he had security clearance, and thus it was he whom the district called one Monday morning. An employee at Fort Gordon had been accused of leaking a single document. Would he take the case? He made the decision casually, right there on the phone. The arraignment would be that afternoon. He had never handled a single case involving national security law, but he was on the list and said yes, so he was Reality's attorney.

In his office, Nichols received an automatic email saying that the indictment had been unsealed. He thought this was odd, melodramatic; this was not a case, so far as he knew, that involved "Chinese spies or nuclear secrets." He drove over to the courthouse to meet his client, who was being held temporarily in the courthouse jail. She was wearing an orange jumpsuit, shackled, behind glass for the moment, but he knew she would be free soon, out on bond. He picked up a big black phone.

"What's your name?" he asked her. And then, "What's your real name?"

To Titus this was a "basic case." Some girl working for some contractor had leaked a single document. At the arraignment that afternoon, he met Jennifer Solari, the assistant U.S. attorney. Solari was, like him, a former military lawyer. She was slim, her hair cut sensibly. She had been a military prosecutor and a special agent with the Naval Criminal Investigative Service, had graduated first out of 216 students at the University of Georgia's law school.

She was a woman who thrived in institutions, and her role here, at which she would excel, would be to cast any deviation from institutional conformity as bizarre and threatening, *unusual*. Titus's focus now was the same as Billie's, as Gary's, as Brittany's: get Reality out of jail, back home, on bail so they could untangle all of this together.

The arraignment began on Monday afternoon at 3:29 and ended at 3:41, twelve minutes in which Billie and Gary and Justin and Wally and Titus gathered in a courtroom to face the judge. It was June, and the last time Billie had seen Reality was Christmas. She had been hoping to hug her daughter. But Billie was seated on one side of the courtroom, and when her daughter entered she was in shackles and a jumpsuit, on the other side, guarded by two U.S. marshals. The judge asked Reality if she had ever been diagnosed with a psychiatric disorder, and Reality said "bulimia," which was the first Billie had ever heard of it. Billie began to cry. *I love you,* she mouthed to Reality, but she wasn't sure Reality saw.

At the mention of bail, Solari was elusive; Nichols didn't understand it. *No one has been shot,* he thought. *No one is dead. It's a document!* The prosecutors asked to have a few days to look into the possibility of bond. They would meet again Thursday, and after that, Billie hoped, she would be able to touch her daughter.

Titus returned to his office. It was 5:00 P.M., hours after he had accepted the case. He had other cases to attend to. His phone rang, and the caller was from *The Washington Post*. "I just want to get a comment from you," said the journalist, "in regards to the attorney general's press release."

"What press release?" asked Titus.

"You haven't read the press release?" asked the journalist.

Nichols googled *Reality Winner press release* while still on the phone, and skimmed it: *federal contractor, mailing classified material, threat, national security, held accountable.*

"At this time no comment," he said. He had no idea why the case he had accepted on a whim that morning was of interest to the attorney general of the United States. Between 4:30 and 9:30 the phone continued to ring, asking him questions he could not answer, because as of yet he had little more information than the journalists themselves. He had seen none of the evidence. At home, his wife wondered where he was.

It was a CNN reporter who first said the word *Russia* to Billie. "Russia?" she asked, thinking he was mistaken. She had thought it would be something having to do with the Middle East. She'd never heard Reality mention anything at all about Russia. She turned off her phone for a while. She needed to think. The next time she picked it up, the caller was Rosie O'Donnell. She wanted to express her support for Reality. Was there anything she could do?

Outside Reality's little brick house, the sparsely furnished rental in the bad neighborhood, the place Billie had found in disarray after FBI agents had torn through stacks of books looking for evidence of treason, reporters had started to gather. Billie heard them outside the windows, behind Reality's squat little Nissan Cube. There was someone from AP, someone from NBC News, someone from News Channel 6.

She's a good person, Billie and Gary said over and over. *She's dedicated to making the world a better place.* A veteran, a volunteer.

CNN invited Nichols on to discuss the case, which he agreed to do, and where anchor Erin Burnett immediately confronted him with one of Reality's tweets: "the most dangerous entry to this country was the orange fascist we let into the white house."

"It certainly looks like her politics here are very clear," said Burnett, looking scandalized. Years ago, on Twitter, Glenn Greenwald had accused Burnett of confusing her job with that of a "government spokesperson."

"Erin, that's assuming that that particular social media page is my client's," said Nichols, who genuinely did not know whether it was.

The Southern District of Georgia doesn't keep its own prison; it pays other prisons. And so Reality was kept ninety minutes away, in the town of Lincolnton, Georgia, a perfect circle of a city that extends in a one-mile radius around a single point, and at that point, a monument to the Confederacy. There were seven other women already there, all on drug offenses, all in a single room with stacked bunk beds.

The television was always on, and it was loud, and this was hard for her to take. But frequently during those first few days at Lincoln she saw people she knew on camera. On CNN, she watched Billie and Gary, seated stiffly beside each other and staring into the camera. Their interviewer was, incredibly, Anderson Cooper.

"Billie," asked Anderson, "what has your daughter told you about what happened?" Billie blinked for a long moment. She took in a deep breath. She sighed. "Oh. Um. She um."

Gary grabbed her hand, and held it. "What she told me," Billie said, "was that she was terrified. She was afraid she was going to disappear."

In the days before the bond hearing, Reality's spirits were high. She began teaching yoga to the other women. She would get through these few days by improving the place. She made friends with an inmate named Angie. Reality's phone account wasn't working, but Angie's was, and so it was Angie who called Billie.

"Hey, this is her roommate Angie, but she can hear you, okay? We've seen you on the news, you look nice."

"Oh well thank you, um. Thank you for being so sweet to my Reality. Everybody has been so nice."

"Awww," said Angie.

In the background, Billie could hear Reality shouting. "There are sauces from Belize in the fridge! Tell them to try it 'cause they're really good."

"Okay we will, we will. This is an amazing community. There's so much love and support for you in this community, and all over the world. Reality needs to know people are rooting for her, they're in her corner and—"

"Mom!" laughed Reality. "Stop talking!"

"Some reporters came into the house and took pictures, I hope she is okay with that," said Billie. "Everyone wants to know, who is Reality?"

"That name is cool," said Angie.

Billie started talking about all the support again—the neighbors and family and the GoFundMe a nice lady from Virginia had set up.

"Alright Mom, we are gonna let you go," said Reality. "I love you so much."

"I love you too. I love you too. And we will see each other tomorrow and um I hope we get to bring you home tomorrow night."

"That'd be awesome, girl," offered Angie.

"I love you so much. And Gary loves you."

"I love Gary too," said Reality. "He's the best."

"She says you're the best," Billie shouted.

"Mom," said Reality. "I've never seen him cry before. He cried on TV."

"He loves you with all his heart and we're both so proud of you and nothing in this world would ever change our love and pride in you. You are one of a kind. You are Reality Winner."

"Mom," said Reality. "Have you seen the clip from Colbert?"

"No, what?"

"He opened his show with, 'Well everybody, it's official! Trump is at war with Reality.'"

"I love it," said Billie.

Reality laughed. "I love you so much."

"I love you," said Billie. It was possible that as soon as tomorrow, she would get to touch her daughter.

Angie put her hand on Reality and held her close.

"I'm rubbing her back for you," she said.

"Risk to the community" meant *violence* to Titus Nichols, but that is not what it meant to Assistant U.S. Attorney Jennifer Solari, who arrived on Thursday prepared to argue that Reality was a risk, in a nonviolent sort of way, to the entire country. Nichols was scandalized that he had to even argue for bond in this case. He had seen murderers get bond. He had once represented a bank robber who got bond, and awaiting trial, proceeded to rob another bank.

In the courtroom the marshals had removed Reality's shackles but stayed standing beside her, such that it appeared that this woman in an orange jumpsuit with the word INMATE stitched in yellow across her chest was a flight risk not just later but now, in this very moment. Nichols called Billie to the stand. Billie was prepared to talk about her daughter's lack of criminal history, her service in the air force, and her devotion to the community. They would take responsibility for their daughter, pay her bond, and make sure she showed up for trial. This was Nichols's approach—simply the known facts of Reality's boring life.

"How are you doing today?" he asked.

"Okay," said Billie. "I'm a little nervous."

"This might sound silly," Nichols said to nervous Billie, "but do you recognize the defendant?"

"I sure do."

Reality did not make eye contact. It was, Billie thought, too hard for her to look at her mother in pain.

Nichols asked about her daughter, where she was born, their household, her academic excellence: "top ten the whole way through."

"During her entire time in the military," he asked, "do you know if she ever got in trouble while serving in the military?"

"She never was in trouble, never," Billie said.

Had she ever gotten in any kind of trouble? Well, there was the one time.

"Eighth grade," said Billie, "they were preparing for graduation. It's a big deal. They didn't know if she was going to be the valedictorian or the salutatorian, but they were preparing. And Reality, she—I guess she got her classmates all together, and they—they had the biggest, bestest food fight that the school has ever imagined, and she was not allowed to walk the stage."

Nichols gave the floor to Solari. Billie was still hopeful

that the government would be reasonable. She believed in the United States, took intense pride in her daughter's service to the military. She had raised a woman recruited and commended by the U.S. Air Force, socially engaged and socially responsible. She'd raised a teetotaling liberal scold who spent her free time pushing wheelchair-bound children through marathons. And both she and Reality remained convinced that it would all work out, once these facts were clear and this minor charge was taken care of. As an advocate for children at Child Protective Services, Billie was familiar with courtrooms and proceedings. Reality was not a flight risk. There was no danger in her daughter.

"What's your typical method of communication?" Solari asked.

"She calls religiously. She calls weekly—at least once a week, and we talk at length the one time a week and maybe twice a week."

"Has she ever contacted you through a service called slippery.com?" Solari asked.

"No."

"Have you ever heard of Tor, or the Onion Router, as a software device that would allow you to access certain parts of the internet?"

"No."

"Is it fair to say that, well, ever since she joined the military, she's been trying to deploy to Afghanistan?"

"I don't know if you would say she's been trying to," said Billie. "I mean, in the military, it wasn't an option for her."

"Well, that's what I mean. So was she frustrated that her position in the air force was not going to give her an opportunity to go to Afghanistan?"

"I think, in the beginning, that's one of her—that she had wanted to. But, I mean, very quickly on, she learned that she wasn't going to."

"Isn't that, in fact, why she left the air force, because they wouldn't offer her any ability to deploy to Afghanistan; those abilities were being given to Special Forces–type persons?"

"I don't know if that was the reason," said Billie. "That might have been one of many reasons."

Billie was small and her voice was high and throughout the next years many, many people would underestimate her. But she was not dumb. She was in fact incredibly cagey and deeply opaque, among the most unknowable people I have ever tried to capture in writing. She would not be bullied into Solari's framing, but there was nothing she could do about questions that painted her daughter's desire to travel as vaguely traitorous.

"Did she ever tell you why she took up an interest at the age of seventeen in learning Arabic or Farsi or Dari or any of those?" Solari asked.

"She loves that language," said Billie.

"All right," said Solari, "fair enough. Has she ever discussed with you a desire to go to Pakistan to meet with— I know it's going to sound like a silly question. Has she ever discussed with you a desire to go to Pakistan to meet with leaders of the Taliban government?"

This was the point at which Nichols began to realize how deeply committed the government was to a narrative that had seemed, outside the courtroom, too absurd to contemplate.

"Thank you, ma'am," said Solari.

Billie left the courtroom, badly shaken, and Gary walked in. Gary considered himself a libertarian; in a way, though he was more Republican than Billie, the government's vindictiveness in this case would surprise him less. Gary affirmed his stepdaughter's character, her patriotism, her law-abiding nature.

"You and your wife were largely unaware of what your daughter did in terms of her employment," said Solari. "Is that fair to say?"

"She carried a top secret security clearance," said Gary. "She could not discuss the details of what her job entailed."

"Right," said Solari. "Now, I know you've told the Court—and I understand why—that if your daughter were granted a bond, you are confident she would not violate the terms of her bond, that you know in your heart, you'd bet everything you own that she will do whatever she says she'll do, and she will abide by all the tenets of her release. You would bet everything you've got on that; is that right?"

"That is correct."

"Sir, I have to ask you: Would you have bet everything you had on your belief that your daughter would never violate her oath to properly safeguard classified information?"

"Yes," said Gary.

"You would have believed with all of your heart, based on everything you knew about your daughter, she would not steal classified information; correct?"

"That's correct."

"So it's fair to say that you have been completely caught off guard by the allegations in this case?"

"I am."

Solari came with a story, projected onto the absence of details made necessary by Reality's classified work life.

What the agents found when searching Reality's house, she said, was "downright frightening." There was the issue of all that technology.

"Your Honor," she said, "agents gathered four cell phones, two laptops, and one tablet from the defendant's house in addition to notebooks and other items listed in the search warrant." The agents found "handwritten notes on how to install Tor," which she described as "a means to anonymously access the dark web," which she described as "illicit criminal marketplaces where one could buy or sell classified information, phony identification documents, passports, drugs, weapons, and just about any sort of contraband one could want." They found "a detailed step-by-step plan for unlocking a cell phone to enable her to change the SIM cards," which, she explained, could enable her to transform a phone into "a burner phone that hides the user's identity, usage, and location." There were the diaries. "Amongst the notes about the defendant's new employment with Pluribus International Corporation where she scribbled notes about dental and health insurance, she also wrote, quote, 'I want to burn the White House down.' Other notes: 'Find somewhere in Kurdistan to live or Nepal. Ha, ha. Maybe.' 'Mexico in the spring. Afghanistan in the summer. Asia and Jordan in between.' It seems," Solari theorized, "she wants to be anywhere but the United States.

"As if that weren't bad enough," Solari continued, "the defendant mentions a number of interesting names that drew our concern, if not alarm. Those names were Akhtar Mansour; Mullah Omar; and Mullah Omar's son, Yaqoob. She also mentions Osama bin Laden." Akhtar Mansour, Solari explained, was the leader of the Taliban killed in a U.S. drone strike in Pakistan. Mullah Omar is an Afghan mujahideen commander who sheltered Osama bin Laden and Al Qaeda militants. Yaqoob, she went on, is his oldest son, "second deputy to the new Taliban chief." There were notes, Solari said, that may have been in Dari or Pashto or Farsi that they had not yet translated. And could they trust her to stay in the country? The defendant had "traveled to Mexico various times between August 2002 and August 2006," though she did not point out that between 2002 and 2006, the defendant was a child; she had been there to get cheap braces. Reality perhaps was not herself well financed for travel, but "someone has set up a GoFundMe page for the defendant, which, as of last night, having been up for only two days, had collected $12,415." Julian Assange himself, "international fugitive and founder of WikiLeaks, has praised the defendant via Twitter." And there was the trip to Belize. "By herself for only three days," said Solari. "Nothing criminal about that, Your Honor, but it seems odd to spend the kind of money necessary for a trip all the way to Central America, to go alone, and then to come right back after such a short period of time with very little idea what she did there." If the U.S. could not be the hero of your story, it would frame itself as the Great Satan.

Is anyone listening, Nichols thought, *to the dumb arguments the prosecution is making?*

But who could really know this woman? "The defendant certainly appears to come from some very nice parents who had little, if any, idea specifically what she did for a living, how she felt about it, or why she would steal and disclose classified information," said Solari. "I submit to Your Honor that we have a defendant with maybe a fractured life or a fractured personality. I think her acquaintances and her family know one side of her, the side that teaches yoga and loves dogs and is nice to be around. But as they've admitted, they have no insight into her work life, into her interest as it pertains to travel to the Middle East."

The American state had recruited Reality Winner at eighteen years old. It had taught her obscure languages, knowledge of which it now implied was dangerous. Her wish to use those languages to communicate with people who spoke them in their country of origin was suspicious. The American state had plied her with secrets and access and forbidden her from sharing the details of her work life with those she loved, which, the government now implied, meant that no one could really know her, which meant that she might well have a "fractured personality" unseen to those she loved. The American state had built Reality, and something had gone wrong. But she could not be given back to herself. The risk was too high.

"Reflecting on her character," Solari went on, "is the information we found in her jail calls. The defendant told a woman named Brittany, whom we believe to be her sister, about what she'd done. She said she didn't want to spend the rest of her life in jail and that she was, quote, gonna play that card being pretty, white, and cute; braid my hair and all, gonna cry. *That* is the defendant's character."

This is perhaps the most surprising thing about the story of Airman Reality Winner, linguist, intelligence specialist, a woman who spent years of her life dropping in on conversations among people this country considers potential enemies: It did not occur to her, in a moment of crisis, that someone might be listening.

TRIAL EXPERIENCE

Moments after *The Intercept* published the document found in its P.O. box, the FBI released a story of its own about a woman named Reality Winner, whom it had arrested days before. A staffer remembers reporters sitting in silence on a couch. Someone had scotch. The TV spots were canceled. There was a time when you could look at a classified document and convince yourself it had been taken without a trace. With the prosecution of Reality Winner, that time period definitively closed.

The head of operational security at *The Intercept,* who had not been consulted at any point from the moment the document arrived to the moment it was posted for all to see, was in Iceland with his wife, en route to Europe at the start of what might otherwise have been a restful vacation. He would find on social media, the morning after the document was posted, a slew of angry strangers blaming him for the failure. *The Intercept* was called incompetent in *The New York Times* and *The Washington Post* and all over Twitter, not only perhaps because it had been, but because it had repeatedly positioned itself as superior to the publications that now had the job of explaining the indifference shown toward a source. What happened next would be called by Laura Poitras "a cover-up" of "egregious source protection failures" but to the rest of the world was simply silence. The staff was told not to talk to the press.

The Intercept released a statement it called "Statement on Justice Department Allegations," authored by, mysteriously, *The Intercept*. "While the FBI's allegations against Winner have been made public through the release of an affidavit and search warrant, which were unsealed at the government's request," read the statement, "it is important to keep in mind that these documents contain unproven assertions and speculation designed to serve the government's agenda and as such warrant skepticism. Winner faces allegations that have not been proven. The same is true of the FBI's claims about how it came to arrest Winner.... We will make no further comment on it at this time." This and further statements from *The Intercept,* none of which would lay out the sequence of events that led to Reality's arrest, took on the self-important vacuity of the secret state the publication had been designed to penetrate. Here was a statement about not stating, expressed in deflective syntax reminiscent of the NSA itself.

The prosecution was ready to bargain; they offered sixty months, five full years in prison. Reality said no. Nichols appealed in the bail hearing in the hope that its absurdity would become clear with time. He was joined by a white partner in the firm for which he worked, John Bell. John Bell was sixty-eight at the time. He wears tiny wire spectacles. His hair sprouts large and fluffy from the sides of his head, but not the top. When he says the word *government* it sounds like *guv'mint*. When he says the word *brutality* it has four quite distinct syllables: *bru-tal-i-ty*. "Well let me tell you the history" is the alarming way John Bell begins answers to simple questions. "Let me explain somethin'," he says again and again.

"I bought yer book," he said the first time we had a real conversation. "Started readin' it. You're a complicated writer. Go read some Hemingway! Double negatives. Obscure. All the big words."

"I think you know those words, John," I said.

"Hm. Maybe."

John Bell has something increasingly rare, which is trial experience. He stayed on the indigent list—the list Nichols was plucked from, the list kept in place of a public defender's office—to accumulate such experience. He is good with a judge. He knows them all. He knows how to perform humility, self-deprecation.

John Bell had no experience at all with Espionage Act cases. What he knew was the jurisdiction, the people. He knew about juries. He knew, for instance, that while well-off white jurors were unlikely to be sympathetic to a poor victim in a personal injury case, they may well decide against a chemical company responsible for contaminating water, because they tended toward great respect for property rights. He knew that a certain kind of working-class jury member, cigarettes in his pocket, oil on his hands, "ain't particularly concerned about niceties of groundwater pollution," which is to say, might side with the company.

The Intercept issued another statement, this one from editor Betsy Reed, who took responsibility for "this failure," though the failure itself remained mysterious. "At several points in the editorial process," she wrote, "our practices fell short of the standards to which we hold ourselves."

No one was fired. No one stepped down. The staff had been told that they could not talk about the case, and so it could seem to journalists completely unrelated to these mistakes that they were required to share in the blame for them. There were dozens of full-time journalists on staff, and yet from the outside it could seem as if the entire publication was synonymous with the careless actions of a few people. It could also seem that the publication was synonymous with its loudest voices, one of which persistently denigrated the importance of Reality's leak and did nothing at all to raise her profile.

"I never liked the story," Greenwald told *New York* magazine. "I thought it was bullshit and knew it was going to be huge in a way that was totally unjustified in what it actually revealed. I think it tried to overstate the importance of what that document was."

It would prove extremely unfortunate for Reality that the audience who might be most interested in and moved by her case was largely captured by a publication embarrassed by it. But where there was not much awareness-raising, there was cash. In the "mistakes were made" statement, Reed announced that First Look, *The Intercept*'s parent company, had "taken steps" to "provide independent support" for Reality's legal defense. The fight would thus not be the DOJ versus the Winners, who lived in a trailer in a town of which no one had heard. The fight would be the DOJ versus, essentially, French American billionaire Pierre Omidyar's willingness to spend. First Look would, in the end, spend $2 million. They hired Baker Donelson, a slick firm with twenty-two offices, 650 lawyers. "So many lawyers!" said Bell. They had lawyers who had defended espionage cases and they had lawyers who had prosecuted Espionage Act cases. They had lawyers who knew the government from the inside, because they had been assistant attorneys for the DOJ, just like the people who would prosecute Reality.

Baker Donelson would now work with the local counsel, Bell and Nichols. This partnership would be messy. Lead among the Baker Donelson lawyers was sixty-seven-year-old Joe Whitley, an insider's insider, a man who had served in the DOJ under four different presidents. After George Bush established the Department of Homeland Security after 9/11, he appointed Whitley its very first lawyer, which is to say Whitley had been the man defending the agency that was supposed to protect us from the kind of person the prosecution would like us to believe Reality was.

Bell didn't have those credentials. He had trial experience, which he assumed the other lawyers did not have. This seemed, to him, a relevant distinction. "I sent out an email to all the counsel," he says, "and said we all kinda workin' togetha for the first time, I think we all oughta share with each other our trial experience."

No one responded. But Bell says he did get a phone call from Whitley, who, according to Bell, called the email "the most offensive thing I've ever seen someone do." Joe Whitley has declined to speak on the record, but, in a statement, writes that Bell and Nichols were "involved in every material decision affecting the case throughout its pendency," and "As is common with teams of lawyers, there were, from time-to-time, disagreements or differing opinions on strategies—what motions to file, when to file them, what defensive avenues to pursue, and the like. These internal deliberations, in our view, are confidential." Bell suggested they should be thinking about a mock trial. Again, crickets. Bell suggested they all go to dinner. "No John, I'm really tired. I think I'm just going back to the hotel," he recalls hearing. "And then the next day in court they talkin' bout a restaurant four blocks from my home where they had dinner!"

"They thought of him as country bumpkin local counsel," says Nichols. But Nichols didn't have ego in it. "My role is okay I am a thirty-something-year-old Black lawyer who is sitting at the table in one of the biggest cases in the country. This is a big deal! I honestly do not care if Baker Donelson is including me in their cockamamie ideas."

It was hard to coordinate on ideas, cockamamie or otherwise, because the classification restrictions placed on the defense were enormous. Indeed, having clearance meant that Reality's lawyers were far *more* restricted than the average person. We can access the document Reality leaked, now available on *The Intercept*'s website. The lawyers could not access it, because they had security clearance, and to access improperly shared material would be a violation of clearance. They could not discuss the case on the phone, unless it was on a secured line, but they did not have secure lines. They could not email about the case unless they had secured email, which they did not have, though the government did. They were in Augusta, Atlanta, New Orleans, Tennessee, and Washington, D.C. They could all fly in and meet in an approved Sensitive Compartmented Information Facility, a windowless room either constructed or renovated to resist surveillance, or they could schedule times to be at individual SCIFs and speak to one another. This required getting security clearance, of course, but also getting approval to use any particular SCIF—which might take months—and then scheduling time for that SCIF when the other lawyers were also available. They asked the court if they might call one another from secure lines in separate SCIFs; the court said no. If they wanted to bring Reality into the conversation, there was yet another obstacle. She was ninety minutes away from anything, because Augusta outsourced the responsibility of holding federal inmates. So she had to be bussed ninety minutes to Augusta, ninety minutes back. This had to be scheduled with the sheriff's office at a time when they had a bus, staff, and security available.

What was most maddening about this, at least to Nichols, is that there was virtually no information of any interest that they were actually protecting. It seemed to him to be a series of pointless logistical obstacles. "I have not learned anything I didn't know in this case that I didn't learn reading Yahoo News the day of," said Titus. "I would watch television and say 'Oh, that's new! I didn't know that happened.' And then I would learn that it's related to my case. But because it's national security, we all have to pretend we're dealing with nuclear secrets. You literally could go on Yahoo News, read a summary and you'd know all the facts that I know in my case. We couldn't even do Google searches. The government said if you Google-search a certain combination of words, someone monitoring you would know what you're referring to. It's international news! I don't have to Google-search it. All I gotta do is watch *Good Morning America.*"

In court, everything was treated as if the smallest revelation would bring the end of a nation. In a meeting during which the judge pressed for hard deadlines from the defense, and the defense pleaded that they could not give dates because most of the lawyers on the team were sixty to ninety days away from security clearance, and thus did not have the ability to even look at the documentation with which they might defend their client, and also had not the slightest clue how many relevant documents they would encounter once cleared, the prosecution provided this information: "The information that I have been cleared to provide in an open setting about classified discovery is that the government agency has produced approximately 400 pages in classified discovery."

A crisp young Baker Donelson lawyer named Matt Chester explained that there would be need for experts, and to request more information that the government had not made readily available, and so on, but the judge was skeptical of the lawyer who did not yet have clearance to look at the client's case and would not, even when cleared, have permission to Google the document she had leaked, which was publicly available on *The Intercept*'s website. "You know," the judge said, "at the heart of this is just a fundamental disagreement about how you approach litigation. My approach and my requirement here is that we set specific deadlines." And deadlines were set.

Billie had been warned by the lawyers to avoid media, and as a social worker, she had always declined interviews. She was not political and was wary of this kind of attention, where it was so easy to say the wrong thing and impossible to know how something might be spun. But she had seen with her own eyes, in court, what happened when the DOJ was allowed free rein to tell its story. When Reality appeared on network TV she was mocked for the name her mother had given her and dismissed as a joke. On right-wing media, where there was time to elaborate, Reality was slammed as a traitor, savaged for her appearance, and characterized by her social media posts. "Reality Winner Hates Trump, Hates Whites—Loves Iran?" ran a headline in *The Washington Times*. No one else was going to tell the story Billie wanted told.

Billie would schedule a rally in Texas, the intention of which was to tell the true story of Reality Winner: pamphlets, postcard signing. She called the Knights of Columbus and asked to use their hall for an awareness-raising event for her daughter, who had been imprisoned. It was hard to get an answer. What was this about, exactly? Billie was realizing that this was not, to a skeptical audience, an easy story to tell. The managers of the Knights of Columbus Hall in Kingsville would "have to ask the board" for permission. She called the manager of the local strip mall, where the Tractor Supply and Hobby Lobby sat across from the high school at which Reality had been mascot. Could she do an awareness event in the parking lot? It was a place she had seen people selling cookies, doing car washes, and it was perfect in that on a Saturday there was no busier place in town. Absolutely, the manager said. Not a problem. Billie was elated; this was a spot far better than the KC Hall. She drove an hour to Corpus Christi to print out packets of information, as there was no printing shop in Kingsville. On her way back, the mall manager called, irate. Billie had lied, according to the manager. She had new information that there would be "busloads" of people at this "protest," this "major march." "No ma'am," Billie said many times. "I did not lie to you." Billie, the mother of a girl who had been accused of espionage, was discovering that the military town that had raised Reality would not be a bastion of support.

It was three days before the event, with nowhere to hold it. Billie frantically called every venue she could find. Kingsville Parks & Rec would consider the event, should she be able to come to a meeting with park management and convince them. She had to sell them on it, and she did.

On a Saturday afternoon in June twenty people, most of them known to Billie through her work at CPS, ate hot dogs in the sun and flipped through the stapled packet Billie had had printed in Corpus Christi. Headings on it were ESPIONAGE ACT and DEFINITION OF THE ESPIONAGE ACT and WHAT IS THE ESPIONAGE ACT. At the back of the packet was a kind of ode to Kingsville that Reality had handwritten from jail. "What hometown is ever large enough," the letter asked, "to contain the ineffable ambitions of the teenage heart?" They were in a spot deep in a park that was itself near nothing. No one would see the rally who was not already committed to supporting Reality. It was not at all what Billie had hoped.

Billie moved into Reality's rental home in Augusta, the one at which Reality had been interrogated, the one that FBI agents had ransacked for Billie to clean; from here she could visit Reality in prison, and they were more likely to win an appeal on bail if Reality had family in the area. The little home was so empty. Reality had never been much interested in things. As a mother, Billie liked things. The family had a rule at Christmas. Everyone gets four presents: *something you want something you need something to wear something to read*. But Billie could never limit herself to so few presents. Brittany and Reality would see the tree and say, "What happened to four things?"

Billie began volunteering with Paws to Hands, the rescue from which Reality had gotten the neglected collie mix, Mickey, who had been reclaimed when Reality was arrested and placed with another family. Billie went to an event where several rescues were fundraising, and bonded with a three-legged pit bull.

I'm not in a position to adopt an animal, she thought that night, back at Reality's house. Her days were full of calls with lawyers, journalists, and feuding supporters who had different ideas about strategy. She was learning about the American prison system and she was learning about American media.

"I don't need him," she thought, "I already have a dog with me," which was true; she had brought another rescue dog up from Texas. And then: "I don't need him but maybe he needs me."

The next day she thought: "Maybe I do need him." She told Cherish, the woman who ran the dog rescue, that she would adopt him. His name was Outlaw Babyface Nelson. For a few months it was just Billie and her dogs, until Billie received another call from Cherish. Cherish employed, at her rescue, former inmates who could not find jobs elsewhere. There was a twenty-six-year-old woman named Jessica who was about to move out of her halfway house, but because she had a felony conviction, could not find a place to live. If Jessica could not find a place to live, she would have to go back to prison. If she went back to prison, she would once again lose her two-year-old, with whom she had just been reunited.

Well, thought Billie, *I'm not here full-time.* And also, the house had been broken into once, and Reality's camera stolen. Maybe it would be a good thing, helpful, to take a former convict and her baby into the four-room house where Billie lived half of the time. There was the injustice of it, too. *She will lose everything,* Billie thought, *for something she doesn't have the power to fix.* This is how Billie came to be helping a woman named Jessica potty-train her son Marshall in Reality's rental house while a three-legged pit bull looked on. Jessica lived in the rental house for months. Billie charged her $200 and sent that to a fund that would help others transition from the halfway house.

While Billie had sought press, Brittany had been made uncomfortable and resentful by all the attention. She had gotten herself from working-class Kingsville to a prestigious new postdoc at the United States Army Medical Research Institute of Chemical Defense. This was classified science not particularly distant from politics; they were working, for instance, on an antidote to a poison the Russians had recently used to murder a dissident. And so Brittany, in her new life, had to attend periodic "Insider Threat" trainings. Surrounded by a hundred of her colleagues, Brittany watched a bored speaker click through slides that named qualities to note in a peer likely be a threat: Disgruntled. Critical of America. Has connections with foreign governments. Her face grew warm. She wondered if everyone in the room was thinking, in that moment, about her. And while she wanted to disappear she mostly felt angry, ready to confront someone, when the speaker arrived at a picture of Edward Snowden. Would a picture of Reality follow? She thought about what she would do. She would make a scene and storm out. *Fuck you guys! That's my sister.* Though no one ever showed a slide of her sister, the FBI did call the security office at the institute to explain Brittany's family situation. It was not paranoid to feel that one was being watched.

SOMETHING HAS TO BE DONE

Reality Winner was recruited in 2010 and jailed in 2017, seven years in which Americans slowly became accustomed to being tracked in exchange for small conveniences, or simply as the price for engaging in contemporary life. It was hard to turn off the location data on your phone, for instance, and even if you made the effort many apps would continue tracking, so most of us did not bother. It was disturbing to know that the totality of our email and private messages were being scanned by Google and Facebook, but then, we'd already agreed to be tracked by our phones. That a "virtual assistant" you've voluntarily placed in your bedroom would secretly record and send private conversations back to Google was not ideal, but then, Google Nest was already collecting data culled from our thermostats, vacuums were already tracking our floor plans, and we'd long ago accepted that "smart" objects worked better if you just gave up and let them track what they wanted to track. My daughter's babysitter attends the University of Iowa online; I ask her, one day, how it is that she can take tests from her bedroom. "The computer tracks your eyes," she says cheerfully, and on another day, she takes a test from my dining room, and hopes that her frequent glances at the baby monitor don't render her eye movements suspicious. A viral article about a woman who falls in love with a villainous Pharma bro is the talk of the internet for days, on all the sites where we freely surrender our data. Repeatedly embedded in that article is an ad for "butt-flap pajamas"—a red adult onesie with a flap, inexplicably, over the butt. Clicking on this ad triggers the creation of a tracking ID, and the company that created it then shares it with more than a dozen other companies, which pass back further information, cementing a relationship of shared information about the person who clicked on the pajamas. There is no way to undo this; clicking on the pajamas is not a fixable mistake. We are watched always on the internet, and who watches us is not something under our control, or even, in most cases, discoverable to us.

In our time many people are vaguely unsettled by these asymmetries, these incursions into intimate conversations and private space, but very few people resist. It is not the incursions that interest me so much as the speed with which we have accepted them, though I don't know how bad this deal is—convenience for data. Surveillance capitalism doesn't manage a system of jails. It will not kidnap you from your country of origin, strap you down, and pour water down your throat until you break your ribs trying to free yourself. It will not collect the story of your life as an idiosyncratic veteran and frame you, in court, as a Taliban sympathizer. And yet all of this information is potentially available to a state that does have the capacity to do all that. If it can be collected it can be, presumably, subpoenaed.

There will never be a state from which there is no good reason to hide. The radical transparency we have accepted, step by step, these past years, is a bet we have made: that we and the people with the guns and cages will stay on good terms.

Reality and the state were not on good terms and so the state turned time backward and read the indelible history that she, like of most of us, had offered into the ether. The FBI sent orders to Facebook and therefore to Instagram. It called upon Google and called upon Twitter and called upon AT&T and called upon Dropbox, from which it demanded everything in Reality's account along with anything she had deleted. It demanded usernames and credit card numbers and demanded to know precisely when she had logged on, for how long, from where, and with whom she had communicated. From Reality's phone they took photos and a web history. "Something has to be done," John Cage once said, "to get us free of our memories and choices."

The Espionage Act charge is, in itself, a trap. The law does not consider intent, which is to say, whether your intentions were good or your intentions were bad has no bearing on your guilt. The court is permitted to consider whether the document constitutes "national defense information" and whether the accused leaked it. Reality had confessed to leaking it, and so that left Baker Donelson with one defense, really: This wasn't national defense information, because it was well known. In order to argue that, Baker Donelson needed a lot of information it did not currently have. It needed to know what government agencies held. If there was information just like this on the server of the USDA, for instance, accessible to 70,000 employees, they could argue that what Reality had leaked, while technically classified, was public knowledge. In order to know what the government knew, Baker Donelson would have to spend many hours preparing expert witnesses to argue that various subpoenas were necessary, and then hold multi-hour hearings arguing for the issuance of said subpoenas.

Bell wanted a trial, as did Billie. Historically one did not risk a trial with an Espionage Act case, or really with federal cases at all; you pled because the government was unbeatable, and you pled a sentence that reflected the extent of their unbeatability. To someone uninterested in a trial, this was really a negotiation over time. Baker Donelson had several lines of attack, all of them arguably quibbling—but perhaps, in congregate, mitigating. They could argue that the document should never have been classified in the first place, pointing to the very real problem of over-classification. They could argue that this particular piece of information was already well known in the public sphere. The government claimed that the leaked document had caused injury; could it prove this? (The government maintained that it did not have to prove this.) There were some issues of Miranda rights; had she really felt free to stay silent, there in her house, surrounded by agents?

And so Baker Donelson filed. And filed. And filed. Had Reality been free, all this filing would have been seen as an attempt to stall, such that the government would revise down the sentence. But Reality was in prison. It was the government that could afford to stall while Reality suffered. Nichols and Bell suspected that every motion would further antagonize an unsympathetic judge.

Caged inside the Lincoln County Jail, Reality continued to be the kind of person who would order a boyfriend to read a particular number of books a week. She taught yoga to the others, developing a routine appropriate to the small spaces between beds: headstands, twists. She fretted about the low calorie intake of a pregnant inmate, asked her mother to contribute to the commissary funds of the others. Joe Whitley brought her stacks of books. She began teaching herself Latin from a textbook in order to read Ovid in the original; above her bunk, stuck to the wall with toothpaste, was a picture of Nelson Mandela. She is a person who needs quiet, but the room was always loud; she got the women into *Breaking Bad* so she could at least have an hour's peace when it was on. She meditated and whispered mantras: *Inhale suffering, exhale sunlight.* Sometimes they were directed at specific forms of suffering: *Inhale hunger, exhale for families in Syria.* "I try my hardest," she told a new friend over the phone, "to believe that it helps." When she saw the pregnant inmate smoking a cigarette, she grew enraged, and told her mom she would never help her again. She was going to keep to herself now, she said, though of course that was not true.

Visitation was thirty minutes, one visitor at a time. Billie and Gary split their time into twenty- and ten-minute increments. All her mail, in and out, was read, and she was not allowed to receive magazine articles. Billie discovered, with time, that she could send Reality a magazine article if she also handwrote something on it, because that was considered "a personal letter." They were coming to know the unspoken rules of the place.

During Bible-study sessions, Reality asked so many challenging questions of the instructor that the others began to see her as a useful distraction; they could get some extra sleep while she took up the teacher's time. In letters to friends and family and to me, she threw side-eye to her captors. "I hope this finds its way to you expediently," she wrote me, "—looks at the vague, yet menacing government agents—"

Reality was only allowed to see people for those few minutes on Saturday and Sunday mornings, and the people she saw, friends and family, had to be on a list of nine that she gave the jail in advance. In September, in a letter that included a hand-drawn heart under the valediction PEACE AND LOVE, Reality agreed to add me to that list, and a few weeks later I flew to Atlanta and drove three hours to the small town where she was being held.

Attached to the Lincolnton courthouse, described by the state tourism board as "in the neo-classical revival style"—behind it and not visible from the road, in what is best described as "riot-proof institutional"—is a one-story brick box lined with wire fencing. The jail is attached to a fenced concrete platform topped with coiled barbed wire, which I recognized immediately because I had seen it in pictures of Reality published on TMZ under the headline "Reality Winner Still Working Out Behind Bars."

On the Saturday morning in October when I came to visit Reality, the day was bright and warm, but through a set of double doors, in the fluorescent-lit waiting room, weather ceased to exist. A guard behind glass took my license through a slot, checked it against Reality's visitor list. She led me into a narrow room and disappeared.

Reality and I spoke between glass on thick black phones tied to the wall by silver cords. She smiled shyly and spoke in complete sentences aphoristic in their tidiness. She was disappointed because when she had asked on Friday to go outside to have her allotted thirty minutes on the concrete platform surrounded by electrified wire, she had been told no. There was no outside time on weekends, so she would have to wait until Monday to ask again for the privilege of natural light. Alone in the room, on a recorded line, we talked, for a few brief minutes, about Kingsville, life in captivity, her father.

"He never shied away from ideology," she said of their post-9/11 conversations. "Even though we were ten, twelve, he told us exactly what they believed."

The guard who had let me in opened the door and began to watch us.

"I had a map of the world above my bed," said Reality, "but I didn't know that—"

"Are you a reporter?" asked the guard.

"What's going on?" Reality said, snapped out of calm into anger.

Forced back into the waiting room, I pleaded with the guard, who never stopped, during our interaction, slowly shaking her head. To talk to Reality, I would have to talk to a sheriff, who was not available and would in any case refer me to the Feds, who would refer me to a byzantine and self-evidently impossible process for obtaining the state's permission to speak to her. That Reality clearly wanted to tell her story was not sufficient reason to let her. Moments after I left, she called her mother. "They're silencing me," she said.

At first, when Billie wanted to talk to media, she asked for permission from Baker Donelson. They always said no. So she said no. She told NBC she couldn't talk. But it seemed to Billie that if she did not talk to media, the other side's story gained power. If she left a vacuum, rumors of treason filled it. Certainly the lawyers were not out there and if one allowed oneself to think too deeply about it, one might remember that the lawyers were being paid by the company that owned *The Intercept,* which was clearly embarrassed by this story, and which had repeatedly insinuated that Reality, not they, was at fault. She began to ignore their advice. It was important, she discovered, to tie Reality's story to the news of the day, whether it be about Russia or Trump or Snowden. It was important for her to be on social media every day, looking for opportunities to insert Reality into the broader conversation. The two times she got Reality trending on Twitter, it was thrilling. People were noticing. Sometimes the lawyers called her, and told her to stop.

"I pretty much found out," she said later, "that it was better to do what I thought was right and what I thought was needed and have them yell at me. I would act and then go *oops, all right.*"

Billie was not the mother Reality had expected. She had expected "you fucked up, but we still love you." But Billie quickly discerned an entire broken structure: a military and a prison system and a culture of secrecy that punished good people.

A jail is a temporary place you're meant to stay for a night or a week before trial. It is not meant to hold someone for months and months. This wasn't, in the end, *Orange Is the New Black;* there wasn't a GED program, or a cafeteria, or a commissary where you could buy makeup. There was one room and in that room women in various states of crisis.

The days were long and boring and yet unpredictable. She lived only for the thirty minutes a day she got outside, but she was often denied those thirty minutes without explanation, and on those days she was devastated. Food was a constant problem; there was no fruit, not a single healthy item for someone who had been obsessively healthy days previous. She ate peanut butter and oatmeal, mostly. The vegetables she got were canned peas and corn; they were salty, and the salt made her feel ill. Her skin became wan and acne-ridden. She felt sick all the time. She talked to her sister on the phone frequently, and to her new friend Wendy, a liberal supporter in Florida who soon became Reality's most important connection outside her family. They talked, sometimes, four or five times a day.

Her lawyers appealed the bail decision. It was, after all, extraordinarily rare for someone charged with the Espionage Act to have to await trial in prison. There was precedent to which to appeal, and the fact that no evidence had emerged to tag Reality as a terrorist.

Solari's first witness was Justin Garrick, the FBI agent whose rescue dog had chewed through three Apple power cords, "ninety bucks a pop." He had been through her diaries, her notes, the parts of her mind she had made manifest.

"Did you come across any handwritten notes that were of concern?" asked Solari.

He had. There was a handwritten note: "I want to burn the White House down. Find somewhere in Kurdistan to live or Nepal. Ha, ha. Maybe." There were notes, too, about changing the SIM card. About downloading Tor, through which Garrick explained "someone can access not only the internet, but also the deeper, dark web on a completely anonymous level." On her computer, they found a burner email account from something called Slippery Email.

"When taken in its totality," Garrick said, "it appears as though it's a covert communications package or could be one." He had found notes about the Taliban. A note in reference to two Taliban leaders that said, "They both understood the need for peace, yet were pushed too far by western demand for unconditional surrender." Another said, "Perhaps Bin Laden was the Judas to Omar's Christlike vision of a fundamental Islamic nation."

She had searched, on her laptop, for the Twitter account of a Taliban spokesperson. Garrick found handwritten notes on "specific identifying information related to foreign intelligence targets associated with terrorism activity," though Solari indicated he could not say more because it was classified. She had searched for flights to Jordan and Erbil. She had searched home prices in Jordan. She researched work visas in Afghanistan. She had searched information about the Taliban, written down her thoughts. They had found the text messages to Brittany. "I only say I hate America three times a day." "I have to take a polygraph . . . #gonnafail."

"So you're on Assange's side?" Brittany had asked once, via Facebook messages.

"Yes, and Snowden."

John Bell cross-examined Garrick. Things would move a bit slower now in the courtroom.

"Agent Garrick, you take your job quite seriously, don't you?"

"Yes, sir."

"And, certainly, in something such as counterintelligence, that's a very important area of FBI work today, is it not?"

"Yes sir, it is."

"And you, certainly—when you do report, you want to get the whole story and not just pick and choose little bits that might give a very inaccurate picture. You agree, don't you?"

"Yes."

"And I bet you've even heard that famous old Ben Franklin phrase that half a truth can be a whole lie. Is that correct? Are you aware from looking at the various documents she—and her mail, and everything else in her house—she has expressed interest in the Peace Corps?"

"Yes."

"But you didn't mention that?"

"No."

"And you don't think it's anything questionable for a person—American citizen or veteran honorably discharged serving their country—to want to go work for the Peace Corps and perhaps help the less fortunate in a foreign land?"

"Correct."

"And you did not mention that, did you?"

"No, I did not."

Bell did this to Garrick over and over. Did he think Doctors Without Borders was a terrorist organization? Did he think Bell's own son, who owned many cell phones for his job at NBC, was doing something wrong by frequently changing his SIM card?

"Now, do you have any concern about data breaches of your—things that are on your computer?"

"Yes."

"Do you have concerns that perhaps every time you do Google somebody is recording where you are and what you're looking at and selling that information to others who might have some use of it? Does it concern you that if you look up something, whether it's a car or a mattress, for weeks thereafter you keep getting ads for that particular mattress or that particular type of car on your computer when you just go to Google?"

"I guess it's the way that Google works."

"Okay. They're telling you what you're looking at, what you're doing, where you are all the time. Right? Now if I found that offensive that not Big Brother the government, but big brother Google is watching everything I do and everything I look at on the Internet and I don't like it—is that evidence that I intend to commit a felony in the future?"

"No."

"Is it evidence that I intend to flee the United States and not show up for a court appearance such as I was required to show up for this court hearing today?"

"Do you know how many American citizens have used the privacy they can get from using Tor?"

"I do not have that number."

"Isn't it true that it's in the millions?"

Many objections were sustained in the course of this cross-examination. Bell wanted to talk, for instance, about the film *Charlie Wilson's War*. Did Agent Garrick know the Taliban used to be our allies? What did he know about opium sales? Did he ever wonder what Jesus Christ would think if he were around today? What did he think "espionage" even meant? The judge ruled all of these out of bounds. ("Let's focus on this case," the judge said, "and not so much *Charlie Wilson's War* and the book and movie.")

Brittany had been waiting outside all this time, in a small room with Billie and Matt, Reality's ex-boyfriend. The room was full of drawers and in those drawers pens and knick-knacks and things she joked she would steal. They had not been brought any food, and they had been waiting for six hours. The water fountain didn't push water high enough to drink out of it without licking the fountain itself, and so the three of them had asked for cups, and a long time later, someone had brought tiny Styrofoam ones.

Hungry and tired, she was brought in to help contextualize her sister's life. Brittany explained that the Taliban were "basically, just religious leaders in the Middle East and most of them haven't committed any act of terrorism. It is the rogue people. The terrorist within a normally peaceable organization." The Taliban, she had to explain, fifteen years after John Lindh had gone to prison, was not Al Qaeda. She told Nichols about Reality's commitment to the environment, her "tremendous respect for the earth . . . Both of us agree there are times when we don't use our resources wisely. This is our home. You have to honor it." The sense of humor she shared with her sister: "We have a lot of inside jokes, a lot of things that would look weird outside of our relationship. We just; we're odd. How about that? We assumed it was, you know, a safe place to kind of talk about, you know, our views and things. We used a lot of hyperbole."

The safe place had been the phone. Had been Facebook. Had been texts.

"This was a Facebook chat in which you and your sister discussed her chances of passing the polygraph exam as part of her security clearance," said Solari during the cross-examination. In front of her, Brittany had the transcript of her private conversations with Reality.

"Do you remember that one?"

"Yes," said Brittany.

"And she figured she would was 'gonna fail'?"

"That's what it says."

It was frustrating to Brittany to be asked to recite back, again and again, what was already written for all to see right there. Their conversations, held in a private language so difficult to explain from the hard seat where she sat before a judge and a prosecutor who lacked, it seemed, this sisterly capacity to shift registers. They didn't seem particularly curious about what was meant. They were eager to have her read anew what had been typed, such that it would look as incriminating as possible in this cold context.

"Everything that they do," Brittany told me later, "it's not like science. Where you ask a question and then try to figure out the answer?"

"The court denies the defendant's motion for release from custody," wrote the judge in his denial, less than a week later, "and finds by clear and convincing evidence that no condition or combination of conditions will reasonably assure the safety of the community."

"One need look no further than Defendant's own writings," he wrote, "to surmise that she hates the United States and has plotted against the government. On February 25, 2017, the Defendant wrote her sister that she hated America. When her sister responded with incredulity, Defendant proclaimed again that she hated America. Defendant admittedly admires Snowden and Assange." There again was her "self-described desire to 'burn the White House down.'"

The judge, in this writing, omitted the "ha, ha" that followed the text; later Reality would wonder if she would still be in prison if she had followed up with "lol jk."

"The nature and seriousness of the danger she poses to our nation is high," he assured the court, and she had the financial means to flee the country. The evidence for this was the three-day trip to Belize.

Reality's life was a succession of small humiliations. She was a person who had been stripped of context and thrown into a tiny room. A schizophrenic woman had not been given her medication, though she was begging for it, and punched Reality repeatedly in the face. The punches were not so hard, but the woman's nails were long, and Reality worried about being scratched in the eye, though mostly she worried about how getting in a fight might affect her case, so she took the punches and backed up into view of a security camera.

Once, walking back from a hearing at the courthouse, wrists and ankles shackled, flanked by U.S. marshals, she tripped and fell on her face. The marshals did not help.

A saving grace: unlimited phone privileges. She called Wendy many times a day. She called her sister and her mother. She could turn every violation into a joke. She knew the call was being transcribed, so why not mess with the transcriptionist? "Reeeoooooeee," said Reality, sounding like a high-pitched modem. "Burrrooooooo," said Brittany, sounding like Lilo from *Lilo & Stitch*. Once they had a five-minute conversation in which they just said "vodka" in a Russian accent over and over. "Let the transcript reflect that," Brittany told me. When Wendy got on the phone, they'd often call a third party. Many times, this third party was the White House. "Can I speak to Donald Trump?" Reality said. "This is Reality Winner." It was one of two young women who usually answered. "Stop calling here," one eventually said. She turned Brittany into Google: *Was Pennsatucky also in* Hustle & Flow*? How do ashes turn into diamonds?*

One day Billie came to Lincolnton full of lightness. She picked up the big black phone and looked at Reality across the glass and announced that Brittany was pregnant. The due date, December 4, was Reality's birthday. Reality jumped out of her seat. "I have to get out of here!" she shouted. "My sister is having a baby!"

Sometimes, without explanation, the water stopped running. Often, there was no toilet paper. Reality asked Wendy to come to Lincolnton and steal some toilet paper; with any luck, she could bring the paper with her when she was arrested and forced into Lincoln County Jail. An eighteen-year-old girl called Kay Kay showed up in the prison one day, scared and crying. Reality gave her deodorant, a clean shirt, noodles. She invited Kay Kay to work out with her, but Kay Kay couldn't keep up. To make Kay Kay laugh, Reality put toilet paper on her head and called herself Tupac. She put sanitary pads on her feet and pretended to skate. They became a team. Billie put $200 in Kay Kay's commissary fund and purchased her a book with which to study for the GED.

Wendy became Reality's PR person: She tweeted endlessly and pestered journalists into writing about Reality. Wendy was an interesting case. She had once been married to a man; they had had a little girl. When she was in second grade, the little girl asked if she could go on a date with a boy from her Montessori school. Okay, said Wendy. They went to a restaurant. Wendy and the boy's mom, Deb, sat at a table while the little girl and little boy sat at another table. The relationship between the second graders did not last. But Wendy divorced her husband to marry Deb. Now the two shared five children in Florida.

Prior to hearing about Reality, Wendy had never been terribly involved in anything political, which is perhaps why she allowed herself to become wholly, alarmingly invested in the case of Reality. The injustice of what had happened to Reality filled her days and disrupted her sleep. It became the entire focus of Wendy's life to make Reality laugh. Deb was surprised by this new Wendy, the Wendy who would walk up to Chris Matthews on the street and ask if he had heard of Reality Winner. The Wendy Deb knew had been shy.

Baker Donelson filed and filed and filed again. Reality was ferried back and forth to the courthouse, which she hated, because these were days in which she would not get her time outside. When she was back at Lincoln the women would gather around the television to watch the evening's local news, on which a story about Reality would appear. This story was inevitably accompanied by a color sketch. These sketches looked nothing like her; the face long and hard and mature, the nose aquiline; her youthful moon face replaced with a kind of sinister bony angularity. She grew to recognize the sketch artist in court: big white hair, big bushy eyebrows, a set of tiny binoculars, opera glasses, through which to watch her. He looked, to her, like "Jim Carrey dressed as Mark Twain in *Bruce Almighty*." Once, seated next to her attorney Matt Chester, she felt the sketch artist's eyes on her. She picked up Chester's pen. She stared directly at the sketch artist staring at her. She began to draw.

"No," said Chester.

Her attorneys challenged the confession, claiming that Reality had not been clearly informed of her right to leave the initial interrogation at the house. There was a hearing for this in Augusta, attended by Wendy and Brittany. When Reality walked into the courtroom Brittany saw that her posture had changed. Her shoulders were slumped. She was making herself shorter. Reality was seated with her back toward her sister. Brittany desperately wanted to make her sister laugh. She pretended to cough. When she did, she make it sound like the word *vagina*. Wendy joined in.

Vagina, Vagina, Vagina. Brittany could see Reality's shoulders shaking. She was cracking up. *Vagina. Vagina.* A bailiff came over to Brittany. "If you don't stop that," he said, "I will throw you out of this courtroom."

The lawyers needed more information in order to know what was known. They asked for permission to issue forty-one subpoenas. Everyone waited.

At her twelve-week appointment, Brittany learned that something was wrong. Her baby, a girl, had Turner syndrome. The chances of her surviving were low, but Brittany would cling to that slim possibility.

Very occasionally, Reality called me. She told me that her recent dreams had been of walking, walking, walking. When she got out she thought she would walk across the country. All that open space.

The subpoena requests, Judge Epps complained, were "scattershot, dragnet attempts to find evidence not known to exist." There was of course no other way to find evidence that the government had classified. He rejected forty of them.

Baker Donelson suggested Reality seek a plea agreement. They had exhausted every avenue. Bell did not agree with the decision. Billie, too, wanted her to fight. The uncertainty was hard, and yet it was harder for Billie to accept that her daughter, a patriot, would be labeled a traitor.

John Bell drove up to Lincolnton, thinking maybe he could change her mind. Reality was adamant. The uncertainty, the risk of ten years in prison, was too much. By April she had been in Lincolnton for nearly a year.

In July 2018, one month after Reality agreed to plea, Brittany woke up and felt different. Her fetal Doppler monitor suggested no heartbeat. She went to the hospital and they told her—with condescension typical of health-care professionals, even, apparently, in dialogue with scientists—that she shouldn't use a fetal Doppler monitor, because it would create confusion. But Brittany was right. There was no heartbeat, and there was also no room at the hospital, and so she would have to go home for now, with the fetus without the heartbeat in her womb. Brittany had named her Rowan Leigh. The middle name was Reality's.

The plea deal the prosecution offered was sixty-three months, including time served. That was three months longer than what Nichols had been offered the summer Reality was arrested, prior to almost all of her $2 million, yearlong defense. It would be the longest sentence ever handed down for an Espionage Act conviction. "You can't fight these cases," Nichols told me, "because the government has made it so you can't fight. If you're accused of shooting somebody there are defenses you can bring up. You might be acquitted. If you're accused of disclosing national security, it's so rigged that there's no way you can defend yourself. You're at the mercy of the government just deciding how politically embarrassing this was."

On the eve of the sentencing hearing Brittany and Wendy and Gary and Billie and I met at a Mellow Mushroom in Augusta. Billie took a sip of her IPA.

"I don't like IPAs," she said.

"That's why you don't order one," said Brittany.

Billie began talking about Outlaw Babyface Nelson.

"You didn't need that dog," said Brittany.

"You have a cat with no eyes," said Billie.

It was August in Augusta, and ninety degrees. I was hours early and waited on the steps of the courthouse until we were ushered past the letters from Confederates who would not be able to serve as jurors, up the stairs, into the courtroom. An entire side of the room was dominated by men and women in suits, a show of force from the DOJ. In the back of the courtroom were Reality's supporters: Cian, a man who had dug ditches in Afghanistan that allowed the drone network to flourish, and lived now with the guilt of it, rubbed his hands together nervously. Kathy, from whom Reality had gotten Mickey the dog. Wendy, who always dresses as if about to embark on a vigorous hike, was wearing Merrell water shoes and carrying a Patagonia bag and sitting beside Brittany, who had grown very quiet.

The judge loomed above us. Two armed U.S. marshals walked beside Reality, whose hands and feet were shackled. She was in the orange jumpsuit. Her hair was a frazzled mess, presumably because she was not given a hair dryer. Her skin was pale and splotchy, red in places. Here she was, the center of attention, the reason for the show. She had not been given access to lip gloss, or foundation, the most basic tools with which we prepare ourselves to appear in public. It was a small cruelty in the list of them, but it was a public one; it involved a certain intentional shame.

John Bell, donning a pinstripe suit, had prepared a speech on the broadest theme imaginable: the *im-per-fect-i-bil-i-ty* of mankind. "We have all seen folks including lawyers and bank presidents and even judges do things that they have known they should not have done, and in some cases it reflects an evil and defective heart and sometimes it's just the imperfectibility of mankind. The person before you is a very good person who has done something she should not have done, but she is not an evil person."

Reality addressed her comments to the judge. We saw

only her back as she read, voice shaking. "I would like to begin by expressing my gratitude toward this Court, the Department of Justice, the FBI, and our Government, and sincerely apologize and take full responsibility for my action."

Reality felt as if she were saying goodbye. She had been allowed to surface for a moment; soon she would disappear once again. "To say my father was unique would be an understatement," she said. "A psychology and theology major, he expected us to engage in intellectual discourse by the time we were out of diapers. He taught me some of the most profound and influential insights into our world that undeniably led me to my chosen career. Language became a topic of sincere interest to me.

"I would like to apologize profusely for my actions which have resulted in the damages caused and resources expended by the government and this court, and, in particular, I want to apologize to my family. My actions were a crucial betrayal of my nation's trust."

Beside me Brittany stared straight ahead, shed a tear, and wiped it away. She did not want her sister to remain defiant, not at all. She wanted her sister to do what was smart. But it was as if, in apologizing this way, the way your parents make you when you are a child, she had betrayed herself, and, in betraying herself, she had betrayed everyone else. She was not a traitor, and she knew it, and they knew it. They'd all spent a year of their lives arguing that the leak had been right and just and heroic.

The judge thanked Reality, and agreed to her request that he recommend she be placed at the Federal Medical Center, Carswell, in Fort Worth for the remaining years of her sentence, to be followed by years of supervised release and a lifelong prohibition on profiting from her crimes. This, too, was hard for Brittany to hear. That even when she left prison, she would be surveilled. The nightmare would not just end one day. It lived with them now. It would come home to Texas.

OUR HOUSE

In 2014, a viral video of a Christian woman at a conference ping-ponged about the internet. Her presentation is on the Satanic influence of Monster Energy drinks. She has perfected her argument—that Monster Energy drinks are primarily a vehicle for Satan—into a crisp patter punctuated by forays into Hebrew, textual analysis, paranoid semiotics, and moments of well-timed eye contact. There is in her presentation a genuinely remarkable union of speech and physicality. She is tremendously good at this. "If God can use people and product," she says, folding up an illustrative poster and picking up a can, pointing with crisp and clean gestures that focus the attention precisely where she intends, "so can Satan. You cannot deny that that is a cross." She points to a cross on the can. "And what is witchcraft? When the cross"—meaningful pause—"goes upside down." Here she inverts the can, as if taking a sip. "Bottoms up," she says, tips the can a bit. "And the devil laughs."

Dissidents are moral narcissists—unable to compartmentalize, to ride the wave of whatever mundane evil shapes the lives of their agreeable colleagues. They are difficult and rude and they interrupt and to interview them is to be borne back ceaselessly against the flow of the single narrative on which they have seized. They are crazy in precisely the way it would have seemed crazy as a poor mother in Pakistan, not very long ago, to say that the local doctor giving out free hepatitis vaccines to poor children was part of the Obama administration's CIA plot to capture the DNA of Bin Laden's children—a plot that would lead, in the region, to the deaths of legitimate vaccine providers. It would have been delusional to assume, as an American in 1962, that the sex worker you hired would slip you LSD, after which CIA agents would watch you react behind a one-way mirror, hoping to learn something about rendering American spies immune to Soviet mind control. These stories are unhinged, and of course they are true.

In 2012 Monster Energy Company took legal action against Li Chih, a man who owns a small online forum called "Monster Fish Keepers" for people who love predatory fish, and which costs him money to run. The multibillion-dollar company filed against Dassault (*da-sule*) Wine, on the grounds that someone mispronouncing Dassault might well say *Dassault,* in which case someone looking for a drink called Monster Assault might confuse it with a fine Dassault wine. It went after a pizza chain and a paint manufacturer and initiated legal action against the "Monster Kong nachos" at a Mexican restaurant. Copyright search engine Trademarkia ranked Monster Energy Company its number one "All Time Biggest Bully"; Techdirt suggested the lawsuits amounted to "an avante-garde art piece" on overzealous copyright protection. In various venues at various times Monster claimed ownership of claw marks, the word *beast,* and the letter *M.*

Between 2015 and 2018, five women sued Monster because the corporate culture that created an ethos of bullying fish hobbyists with unprofitable websites was, it appeared to them, not notably feminist. "You have to put up with some things," one of the women suing told Emily Peck at the *Huffington Post*. In a case that eventually went to arbitration, a Louisiana-based regional manager and single mom began dating one of the company's vice presidents; when she tried to call it off, she alleged, he threatened to get her fired. When the single mom tried to report harassment by *another* executive at Monster, the executive she was dating, she said, became incensed. ("You have to have many cocks in you to feel fulfilled," he texted, "I tried every way to get you to look at things different so you would not get written up or fired . . . I bet you fucked 50 guys since I have been with you.") She received a poor performance review, and was eventually fired, for what Monster said were unrelated reasons. In a case that was resolved in mediation after years of litigation, a makeup artist met up with a Monster executive she was dating in a hotel room in Los Angeles for an awards show. A hotel guest found the makeup artist on the floor of her hotel room. There were strangle marks on her neck, according to a police report. Her nails were broken and her thumb was bloody; she said he had bitten her. The company's fruit punch is called Assault. If God can use people and product, so can Satan.

In September 2014, the year the Monster lady went viral, there was news all over social media of a chemical explosion in Louisiana. One could find what appeared to be CNN photos and local news clips documenting the event, and a Wikipedia page referring back to these news clips, though there had been no explosion. If you had said then that government-backed Russians were behind this, and they were practicing for a much larger disinformation campaign that would aid in the election of a reality TV star with narcissistic personality disorder, you would have sounded deeply unwell. You probably would have been.

A prophet of sound mind is no prophet at all. Just look at the can, is what I am saying. You cannot deny that that is a cross. And what is witchcraft but the cross upside down. And what is Satan if not a shape-shifter?

If the Monster Energy lady was prescient in her reading of Satan's hold on a drink, she followed a tradition of fantasy built on solid ground. "Unelected deep-state operatives," Trump had called them, men running secret agencies with secret money, unmolested until someone like Snowden failed to fall in line. Trump pointed to an absence and projected upon it an imaginary world, but his imagination could not contain the place his followers would take the fantasy. At first, the outlines were familiar: These operatives, united against the president, were "globalists" working under the auspices of the UN; the vocabulary was straight out of a *Left Behind* novel, decades tired. By the end of Trump's first term, the fantasy had been rendered new, and baroquely so. By 2020 the participants were not money-grubbing Jews but Satan-worshipping pedophiles involved in what happened to be a matter of obsessive concern for America's police procedurals, which comprised most of its popular television: child sex trafficking. The theories went further. It was not hard to find the claim that Hillary Clinton ate babies, or that furniture retailers sold children.

"A nontrivial 15% of Americans agree with the sweeping QAnon allegation that 'the government, media, and financial worlds in the U.S. are controlled by a group of Satan-worshipping pedophiles who run a global child sex trafficking operation,'" reported the Public Religion Research Institute. And yet with repetition, anything becomes mundane. "There's a once-in-a-lifetime opportunity to take this global cabal of Satan-worshiping pedophiles out," Georgia representative Marjorie Taylor Greene told her constituents, "and I think we have the president to do it." A once-in-a-lifetime opportunity. True believers speak of Satanism with the bored fluency of someone selling condos.

The movement had an anonymous leader, who went by Q, which he said was his clearance level, and the reason he had access to so much secret information about the inner workings of the secret state. Q was a whistleblower. He came into existence because many people had come to believe that the most reliable source of information regarding their government would be a disenchanted insider.

In the claim that the Obamas and the Clintons traded in innocent children, there was an opportunity to feel deeply: the welling horror of indignation, of deep sadness, of clean clarity between good and evil. It felt good to feel. It was reminiscent of something we had lost, between the day the towers fell and the twenty years after, the sense of purpose stripped of enervating ambiguity. QAnon is to its core a positive movement, and has much in common with the kind of insistent optimism that characterizes American charlatanry. QAnon is about making life better, both for yourself and the babies who would otherwise be eaten. The enemy (pedophiles, eaters of babies, the pope) is apparent, and the good guys are winning. There is a plan in place to clear the world of wicked-doing, and an all-powerful president executing that plan. The plan involved "the storm," which was the day when evil would be vanquished and the world restored to patriots and people with normative sexual appetites. On the internet one could find videos about 30,000 sexually abused children who had allegedly been rescued from a network of underground tunnels running from the U.S. and into Canada. The videos were just words over a map showing the tunnels. An alternative architecture.

After a year of growing notoriety among a certain kind of right-wing storyteller, Joe Biggs left his job at Infowars to become an organizer for a racist gang of men called the Proud Boys, beloved by Trump, obsessive about the loosely organized leftist group known as Antifa. He organized a rally called "End Domestic Terrorism," the goal of which was to get Antifa members designated terrorists. Though Antifa was not known to be responsible for any deaths, the FBI got in touch with Biggs, evidently asking for information not about the Proud Boys, but about Antifa.

Biggs had risked his life in Afghanistan, but as the war entered its twentieth year it was hard to find people willing to argue that the thousands of American lives and trillions of American dollars had accomplished anything. He had come to believe that the single purpose of American foreign policy was to install puppets loyal to American oligarchs. A core value for himself and his fans was "being real." A man they perceived as "being real" was Donald Trump. One could not trust the government undermined by Snowden and Assange and one could not trust the media that credulously repeated that government's lies. The principle in which one could believe was *giving offense,* in that giving offense suggested a willingness to make a sacrifice—that of personal comfort—for truth.

John Kiriakou never did get a job at Target or Starbucks or McDonald's. The job offer that did come was from Sputnik Radio, a Russian propaganda network happy to promote someone who presents difficulties for the mythos of American exceptionalism. He took the job. "Remember John Walker Lindh?" Kiriakou wrote in an op-ed. "The word 'treason' was bandied about in news reports of his arrest, and talking heads on the cable news networks talked about a sentence of life without parole for 'aiding the enemy.'" The occasion for the op-ed was the release of John Walker Lindh, twenty years after he had been taken from the fortress in which he had not burned alive.

There was a moment in late January 2021 when it seemed possible to some people that Trump would pardon Snowden, and perhaps Assange, and perhaps even Kiriakou and Reality as a parting gift to the intelligence agencies he despised. That possibility was, for some people, lucrative. Kiriakou was told that Trump's personal lawyer, Rudy Giuliani, would help him secure a pardon for $2 million. He opted to pay $50,000 to another advisor, but neither he nor any of the others were pardoned.

In June 2020, five years free, Kiriakou found photographic evidence that his wife was having an affair with another man at her workplace, the defense contractor Northrop Grumman. Kiriakou sent the photos—in which Heather was wearing a thong, though the extent of her nudity would later be a matter of contention in court—to Northrop Grumman. He was, subsequently, detained for illegal dissemination of photographs; revenge porn. He sued the detective who arrested him. In the lawsuit he argued that he was not motivated by revenge. The affair itself was evidence of waste, fraud, and abuse. His wife and a "high level Northrop Grumman executive" had been "fraudulently billing Northrop Grumman for personal travel to perpetuate adultery costing tens of thousands in business travel." So deeply had Kiriakou internalized the identity of whistleblower that he now claimed he was going after his adulterous wife not out of anger or sadness or desperation but out of a desire to reveal corruption among executives of Northrop Grumman.

A court-appointed psychologist noted the children's "attachment to and affection for" their father, though he had insulted their mother in front of them in ways thought to be "enormously unhealthy" and was "manifesting a worrisome self-justifying position." The psychologist thought the two parents should split custody, and the judge opted instead to award full custody to Heather. Kiriakou did not stop talking. "Coming up next," said Brian Ross in a July 2020 episode of *Brian Ross Investigates*. "A former CIA spy and renowned whistleblower who turned his skills against his ex-wife. You're watching the Law and Crime Network," which you were, if you were a diehard Brian Ross fan, because ABC had fired Ross despite all the Emmys and all of the Peabodys for mistakenly reporting that Donald Trump directed Mike Flynn to make contact with the Russians during the presidential campaign. A colleague of Ross's gave an awkward rundown of Kiriakou's past whistleblowing.

"Tonight's story," Ross said, one imagines, out of embarrassment, "is of much less consequence and significance."

"You were going to Northrop Grumman because . . . you wanted to get your wife in trouble?"

"My wife got herself in trouble," said Kiriakou, speaking from what looked to be a supply closet full of open boxes of paper. There was a garment rack and from it hanging a single black coat. "To me this was evidence of waste, fraud, abuse, or illegality, which is the definition of whistleblowing in the whistleblower protection law."

The two went back and forth into intimate details, awkwardly couched in the vocabulary and mannerisms of nightly news.

"In two of the pictures that were most revealing, I took a sharpie and blacked out the, um." Kiriakou shrugged. "Naughty bits. So there was no porn. There was no revenge. There was no criminal intent."

"Uh," said Ross, "you have it in you just to blow the whistle, looks like."

"I spoke to a psychologist one time," said Kiriakou, smiling, "and he told me whistleblowers have an unusually well-defined sense of right and wrong. Whistleblowers can't help themselves. They have to report evidence of waste, fraud, and abuse. It's just the way we're wired."

"All right."

It was also 2020 when Donald Trump lost an election to Joseph Biden, an election that Alex Jones and Joseph Biggs and many other people assumed to be fraudulent because Donald Trump was a fixed point of realness around which the world turned. "It's time for fucking war if they steal this shit," Biggs posted. In December leaders of the Proud Boys began raising money for "upcoming Patriot events." On Telegram, Biggs helped plan an event at the Capitol, where he and his gang would protest the certification of the 2020 election. "We have a plan," Biggs told the others on Telegram. He wanted to know how many Proud Boys would be in attendance so he could "plan accordingly for tonight and go over tomorrow's plan." Trump was, according to Biggs and many other people, a sympathetic, somewhat hapless patriotic character vulnerable to dark-minded elites who despised him for his honesty. To make themselves real, children invent imaginary friends.

Later, when authorities searched through the communications of people who tried to take the Capitol that day, they would find people who had been living placid, pandemic-constrained lives behind screens and had become desperate for experience beyond the coldly visual. Sometimes, the disease stripped its victims of the ability to taste or to smell. "I wanted to *do* something," a rioter later told me. "I didn't want to just stay home."

Joe Biggs had signed up for the military at eighteen, hyped up to kill for his country, which he did even as he had lost faith in all the institutions that sent him there. Eight months from this day, the American military would complete its withdrawal from Afghanistan, and cede control back to the vicious fighting force with which it had found John Walker Lindh. Just as it had developed dangerous hacking tools it did not have the capacity to keep from malicious hackers, the United States would leave Humvees, helicopters, and surveillance equipment behind in the country it was never able to control. Among the $7 billion of equipment left to the Taliban would be the handheld biometric devices Joe Biggs had used to scan the eyeballs of the dead. "It is unclear," reported *The Intercept,* "how much of the U.S. military's biometric database on the Afghan population has been compromised."

In 2020 Biggs was thirty-seven years old, but looked older. His beard was white. He was heavy-set, substantial in a warm flannel, and in his thick-rimmed square glasses he appeared in the crowd as a kind of hipster grandpa, authoritative and aware, capable of violence but also of irony. He was carrying a radio, and if he had not been trained to lead other men into battle, at the command of the people who made laws in the building before him, he would have seemed ridiculous, a grown man playing at insurrection.

There were barricades around the Capitol. No one had yet breached them. The dome loomed, eight million pounds of precisely cast iron, and standing before the building a handful of cops in Biggs's view: five, six. Behind him were thousands of people who had just heard their president declare the election stolen. "Whose house?" the crowd shouted. "Our house." In the few feet between the packed crowd and the sparse group of cops were some slim barriers, an almost imaginary line between law and lawlessness. A young man in a red hat approached Biggs. No one knows what was said. Immediately after speaking to Biggs, the man bridged the distance. He walked up to the barriers, face-to-face with a cop. He ripped off his jacket with a single swift motion. Turned his red cap around. Shoved a barricade. Started an insurrection.

Hours later, the flimsy barriers were gone, and the Capitol draped in men. Rioters pressed in from all sides spit-shouting sometimes words and sometimes long moans of masculine rage. Hordes of fellow believers packed grand staircases rising upward to the terrace, where men sat on the bannister dangling their legs or hugged lampposts or posed for selfies or lowered themselves back into the crowd.

Men hit the ends of their flagpoles against the ground, *tap, tap, tap,* a steady drumbeat as they marshaled energy toward attack. Inside an arched doorway that led to the interior of the Capitol were baton-wielding black-clad cops in masks and helmets, and standing in a group flanked by marble, behind their shields, they looked inhuman and invulnerable. Three-deep on the steps, surrounded on all sides by screaming men, rioters stomped and heaved and hurled their bodies toward cops. The black-clad force had batons and shields, guns, riot gear against a crowd whose arms were often hidden and sometimes primitive: poles, fire extinguishers, the metal barriers that had failed to keep them out. A crutch, a crowbar, an ax. A metal whip.

A man in a gray coat slammed down the pole of his Trump flag again and again; a man wearing a backpack threw a punch; a man off to the side whacked with a stick, and when the crowd pulled a single cop into itself and beat him with whatever was at hand the cop no longer looked hard but soft-bodied and alone. Twice at the base of the skull he was tased. Panicked police whacked wildly with their batons, sprayed pepper. The mob heaved and a cop, trapped, screamed as the crowd cried with joy and fear. A man beat a cop with a hockey stick. Men tore shields from the police and passed them down the stairs. "Whose house?" the crowd asked. "Our house."

Joe Biggs walked inside the Capitol. "This is awesome," he told someone filming. By the time Joe got to the Senate Chamber, lawmakers had cleared out. In the gallery of the House, old men in slim ties and suits and shiny shoes cowered on the floor, behind folding seats in the balcony. Having lost the line, Capitol police dragged furniture in front of the gallery doors, so angry men with plans would not be able to force their way in. *Oh my God,* thought a representative from Connecticut. *We spend billions and billions of dollars on satellites and guns and weapons and aircraft carriers and artificial intelligence. It's gonna be a freaking desk that saves my life?*

Over the hum of their gas masks the representatives could hear glass shattering, a gunshot, knobs of locked doors rattling. Someone had placed a wooden platform outside the Capitol and on top of that platform a doorway with no door, from which hung a noose. The gallows was symbolic, not functional, though it was not clear, when the crowd shouted "Hang Mike Pence," how much symbolism to infer.

Here was as literal an attack on democracy as one could imagine; an assault on the very act of certifying an election, more direct in its attempt than the attack on financial and military buildings twenty years previous. It was after that first attack that the FBI began handing to the NSA CDs containing billions of American phone records, records that provided a picture of who each American was through the people with whom she communicated. It was after that first attack that Google, Facebook, AOL, and others unlocked the doors to loud rooms full of racks and wire so the NSA could come in and install equipment with which to spy. It was after that first attack that the NSA obtained the ability to record live audio and video and chat, to watch search terms typed into Google. As the rioters knocked on the doors of legislators and staffers wept behind them, American drones washed over much of the globe, sending video to satellites that would send it to receivers stateside, where it would very likely never be seen because relative to its ambitions the deep state is perpetually understaffed.

But on January 7, it would not be the NSA on whom authorities relied to track down the 800 people who would be charged with violating the Capitol grounds.

"We're gonna fucking go in there, life or death! It doesn't matter," Jenna Ryan said from the Capitol she had breached, at which point she turned directly to a camera: "Y'all know who to hire for your Realtor: Jenna Ryan." Somewhere along the way we had lost the knack for anonymity. "My name is Gina Bisignano," said a salon owner from Los Angeles, "Gina's Beverly Hills on Instagram." When the FBI went looking, they would find endless video of rioters livestreaming the act for their followers and at least one Instagram story in a which a rioter posted a picture of himself at the Capitol under a big yellow pointing finger emoji with the caption "This is me." Having found rioters from their own social media posts, they could then turn their attention to fellow rioters those social media users had tagged. The event was among the most filmed in history not because the deep state of which they were worried was watching. Surveillance is made of us.

A RECORD AGAINST MEMORY

"The poem," Wallace Stevens writes, "is the cry of its occasion." A great poem is the poet's cries meaningfully assembled in the discovery of their reason for being, fragments stitched into new knowledge, a communication at its most condensed. Data is the opposite of a poem, countless cries with no occasion, and it is in data that we have immersed ourselves. We are surrounded by information mistaken for knowledge, great wells of fact that gain nothing in their accumulation, treated in courts of law with the gravity of pronouncements etched in stone. All the electrons in the Utah Data Center will not, on their own, tell a single story. There is no meaning to be gleaned from *I want to burn the White House down,* absent the mind that produced it, absent the *ha, ha* that follows it, absent the culture that produced the woman who wrote it.

I have been trying to describe a kind of *thinning*. An heirloom is given its aura of meaning by all that is not passed down. An oral tradition is experience narrowed into something amenable to memory. To will everything to a descendant is to elevate nothing to the status of treasured object. To include a log of every dull detail in the hero's journey is simply to generate noise. This is not a value judgment; many inheritances are unwelcome, and would be better off lost.

We tend to think of privacy as the freedom to keep intentional secrets separate from public knowledge, but privacy has been the freedom to live as if most of what passes for experience will not endure. In the Communications Management Unit of Terre Haute prison in Indiana, known as "Guantánamo North," every word said by John Lindh was recorded by cameras and other listening devices, placed every twenty feet, and sent to a counterterrorism unit in West Virginia. In the service of "managing communications," he and his mostly Muslim fellow inmates were not allowed to speak Arabic outside the presence of a live translator. Lindh rebelled through prayer. He got in trouble for calling for prayer early in the morning. He got in trouble for praying with other inmates, which is forbidden, until he sued for the right to do so and won. He responded in writing to one reporter's questions by declaring that ISIS was doing a "spectacular job," at which point his lawyer dropped him, but when he walked out of prison in 2019, under conditions which forbade an unmonitored internet connection, not even the most motivated among the press could say where he had gone. Still under supervised release, he had slipped beneath public view, and it was possible to imagine for him a privacy remarkably inviolate, a kind of ancient space in which he could pray and remain apart from reality.

Prison is the erasure of personal context and every battle therein is a battle to reclaim it. That Reality Winner was allowed her small space in order to hang a picture of Nelson Mandela was a small mercy in that it reminded her of an identity she had once had, something that put space between her and a caged body with animal needs. Her mail helped, though nothing helped as much as the daily phone calls to Billie and Wendy and Britty. That was what made it possible to get through the long days of small cruelties from the guards and boredom and the endless hours inside. Who was Reality? She was data about data. She was a web of social relationships. A map of connections. To completely sever those connections, which is what the United States did to Abu Zubaydah and continues to do to 80,000 people a day in solitary confinement, induces hallucinations, panic, and paranoia. Cut loose from our concentric circles, we go mad.

After the trial came more uncertainty: When would they take her to prison in Texas? No one told her or her family much of anything. Her lawyers didn't know. She was in the hands of the Bureau of Prisons, an entity that eludes the forces of transparency no less than the NSA, and is in many ways more successful in protecting itself from scrutiny. This is the shadow of shadow America: a network largely beneath notice that resists nearly every attempt to make it knowable. Sometimes prison officials refuse to give information because they claim doing so will threaten the security of the prison, or, incredibly, the privacy of the prisoner. But that is itself unusual, because for the most part, American jails and prisons simply do not respond to requests for information. It is to the benefit of this system's architects that most people do not want to know.

A surprise: Kay Kay was back at Lincoln. She had gotten into some kind of fight with two other girls that was then posted on Facebook. All of the girls—Kay Kay and her enemies—were taken to the jail. Kay Kay was put in front, away from the other prisoners. When the two other girls came in, still talking shit about Kay Kay, Reality pieced together what had happened. She was wearing a federal uniform, different from the others, which gave her an air of frightening authority. They say the most dangerous inmate at the county jail is the one who just got sentenced. Reality had just been given five years. She had a message for the girls.

"If you mess with Kay Kay," she said, "I will scrape your face off your skull."

She repeated this desire—to scrape their faces off their skulls—to the jail captain. "Consider me involved," she said.

The captain told her to calm down. One of the girls would bond out that same day, and when she did, Kay Kay would join Reality in the back.

While Kay Kay was kept up front with the guards, she heard a rumor: They would be transporting Reality that night. But when she was released to the back with the other women, there was no time to tell Reality, because Reality was yelling at her. What was she doing back here? How had she fucked up so badly? Kay Kay ended up in Reality's bed. The two held hands, and cried, and laughed.

The guards came for Reality at 2:00 A.M. A prison would have so much her county jail did not have—a commissary, classes, a real yard and significant time outside—that the word *prison* had begun to contain a kind of hope. It was like she was going off to college. It was not some prison bus, not Con Air, that would transport Reality. It was just the captain of the jail in a government van, driving her someplace. She did not ask questions.

When she and the captain arrived, by early morning, they were not in Texas but in Florida, at another county jail, this one full of undocumented Spanish speakers rounded up and taken in. This was an ICE facility. Reality was put in isolation. She did not have a way to call family, because she did not have an account set up by her family, who did not know where she was.

What followed were ninety-six hours in which Billie had no idea where Reality had gone. She checked the Bureau of Prisons website obsessively, but there was no information, because Reality had not yet even come close to being processed in the federal prison system. No one has ever explained to her why she was taken to Florida.

In solitary, Reality lost it. For well over a year she had not once been alone. She spent so much of her time trying to block out the sounds of other women. Now, suddenly, there was nothing and no one, not a book to read. She wept. She asked to meet with the warden. Why was she in solitary? Why would they not allow her even a Bible? When she was finally able to call her mother, her mother never got the call; they had been having spotty reception in Kingsville.

She called Wendy, sobbing, unwell. It was as if she had snapped. Wendy called the jail. No, they didn't know why she was in solitary. No, they weren't sure whether she could have visitors. Wendy lives in Florida. She got in her car and drove the four hours to the jail. While Wendy was on the road, Reality called Billie and finally got through. *I have no one,* she kept saying, though often Billie could not hear her through the force of her sobs. Billie felt the most powerless she ever had as a mother.

The jail was beige and low to the ground, like a high school, and when Wendy walked in she saw thirty monitors and huddled around each of those monitors families speaking Spanish. There were adults wrangling little kids, pulling them back to the screen to talk to the people who were presumably their parents. This was how they did it here, Wendy gathered; you didn't get glass and a black phone like at Lincoln. You basically got to Zoom, though it was September 2018 and normal people did not know what that was.

Wendy asked the man at the desk whether she could speak to Reality. "Well," he said, "she's in isolation." He said he would "go check" and see whether Reality could see someone. It turned out they could visit by monitor. Wendy was relieved. But when he left and came back again, he reported the monitor in her cell in solitary was broken. They would move her into the next room. But that didn't work either, for reasons Wendy did not understand. It had been an hour of back-and-forth, and now Wendy started to cry; she would never get to see Reality.

The man told Wendy to follow him, and led her to a room with a table and chairs and a phone. "Sit down," he said, but she didn't. She would have thirty minutes. On the other side of a giant pane of glass, Reality appeared, her whole body, head to feet. They both picked up the phone and began to talk until they realized they could hear without it. They hung up the phones and walked up to the window. Wendy put her hands on the glass and Reality put her hands on the glass, but it did not feel to Wendy like glass. It felt to her like human touch. They spoke standing at the glass for thirty, then forty minutes. It seemed the guards had forgotten they were there. "I'm coming back tomorrow," Wendy said an hour later, when the guard came back. Then she drove to a Winn-Dixie and got a six-pack of beer and waffles and syrup and ate alone at a Residence Inn. She had only meant to get involved for a week or two. Maybe a month. She had thought, maybe, she would acquire a pen pal.

Reality demanded to meet with the warden. Why was she in isolation? The warden, who, incredibly, did meet with her, said it was because she had been marked as a "high profile" inmate; she was thus in solitary for her own protection from inmates who might recognize and target her. Reality pointed out that pretty much everyone in the prison was either addicted to methamphetamine or a recent immigrant without English. Did the warden truly think they were going to recognize her? This was apparently persuasive, in that she was let into the "general pop." It was at this point that Reality became upset that there was no Spanish language literature in a jail that largely housed Spanish speakers. Could her mother start a book drive for Spanish language literature? Reality's fans began sending Spanish books to the prison.

The only way to relieve her anxiety was exertion. She asked for cleaning supplies. There were no gloves, just mops and rags. She scrubbed grated metal stairs crusted with dirt and hair; when she started you couldn't see through them, and when she finished, drenched in sweat, you could. Every day, four more stairs. She kept the cleaning supplies until someone asked for them back. A guard gave her a scrub brush; it seemed like a treat.

Ten days after she arrived at Baker County Detention Center she was taken from her bed. She could not keep her Baker County uniform, and Lincoln had lost the clothes in which she had first gone to prison, and so she traveled in long johns, on a plane. She was flown, mysteriously, back to Atlanta. No one explained why. From Atlanta, she was taken to a processing center in Oklahoma. The processing center was over capacity. She was bussed to another Oklahoma facility.

It had been weeks since she was taken from Lincolnton. Here, in Oklahoma, there was filth as she had not seen before. There were ninety women in a room. Two toilets so close together your thighs could brush another person's as you used one. There was a single shower with four showerheads, but due to the Prison Rape Elimination Act of 2003, only one of those showerheads could be used at a time. There was, therefore, an ever-present endless line of people waiting to get to the shower, though the line was nominal; in order to know how long the wait would be at any given time, one had to find the person standing next to the shower, ask who was behind them, find that woman, ask who was behind her, and so on, until one reached the end or gave up hope.

She had somehow crossed the country and yet not been outside in eighteen days. Reality grabbed a dirty rag and a bottle of bleach and in the spaces in between women, she started to clean, to attack the filthiest corner of the room. A guard stopped her. Only state inmates, she said, were allowed to clean. Federal inmates could not.

By November 2018 it had been 700 days since Billie had touched her youngest daughter. That was the month Reality called and said Billie could come visit her at the Carswell Medical Center, where Reality had finally landed weeks before. Visitation was at 8:30 on Saturday morning. Billie printed out a twenty-two-page PDF of rules the prison provided about visits. She read them very carefully; she knew from her year of dealing with Lincoln that any small violation, however unintentional, could cancel a visit. "The rotation is based on the fifth digit of the Register Number," the rules said. The fifth number of Reality's rotation number was odd, and so between April 15 and October 15, she could have visitors on Saturdays but not Sundays, though the rules were different for holidays. The rules said only two adult visitors would be allowed at a time. Billie was not permitted to wear close-fitting pants, or pants with holes, and Reality was not permitted to wear running shoes. "Proper undergarments must be worn," the rules said. If Billie made it through the gauntlet, she would be allowed to greet Reality with a hug. From the moment she printed out the rules, she was a ball of worry. Her need to touch her daughter was totalizing.

Billie placed the twenty-two pages in the backseat of the car. She and Gary drove the eight hours to Fort Worth and stopped for the night at the Holiday Inn. Billie checked the GPS many times: fourteen minutes from the hotel to the prison. They would leave an hour early. Gary thought it was too much time, but Billie insisted.

They left the next morning at 7:30. She had with her precisely six dollars' worth of quarters in a transparent plastic bag. They drove past run-down homes with patchy lawns, a nicer neighborhood with trees and gates, past blank warehouses and churches. The land was that flat open Texas scrub, no sidewalk to delineate street from grass, just the gradual petering out of green in transition to cracked blacktop. Ten minutes into their drive, the houses were fewer and fewer until the land was not lush exactly, but thinly forested. They passed a Girl Scout camp. From a clearing three deer watched the car pass.

Fourteen minutes into the drive that was supposed to be fourteen minutes they saw, on their left, a metal fence topped with barbed wire, and behind that a concrete fence topped with coiled concertina. Just above both fences was the flat beige institution that must be the prison. On their right, trees. But they could not find the entrance to the prison. They saw no signs, only the fence that extended onward as they drove. They turned around after they'd passed it, and turned around again and again, taking wrong turns that drove them further from Reality. Now it was 8:00. There did not seem to be any way to get from the road they were on—Meandering Road, it was called—through those fences. Billie's hands were sweaty. She checked the pages she had printed out, but she knew they said nothing about how to get from the road to the prison entrance.

On Meandering Road they had passed a sign that said NAVAL AIR STATION. They backtracked to the sign and drove up to a little security post, where two friendly uniformed sailors tried to help. They knew of the prison but not how to get in. Billie was fully panicking. It was 8:20. Billie called the prison, not expecting to be helped, really, not knowing whether anyone would even answer. But the person who answered mentioned a lake that they had seen, and that was enough for Gary to finally find his way. There had been a small sign that said BUREAU OF PRISONS that they had repeatedly missed, which led to what looked like an apartment complex, but was actually a road that led all the way around the perimeter of the prison, and finally to what looked like a service entrance. A friendly man in a khaki-colored uniform asked them who they were there to see. Reality Winner, he said, was not on his list. They waited as he called the prison. He gave them forms to fill out in their car. They had a pen in the car, and if they had not had a pen, this would have been a problem.

By 8:30 they were through the second gate, but this gave them no time to lose as they found their way in. They didn't know where to park. It was not just the pressure to see Reality; there was this sense Billie had around prisons, that if you did something wrong, you too would be imprisoned. The stakes were different here.

They parked—it would turn out later, in the wrong place—and walked into a building carrying their paperwork and six dollars in quarters in a transparent plastic bag. When they came in, no one else was waiting; they were so late that everyone else had gone through to the visitors' area. The woman at the desk did not even look at them. Billie said, "Excuse me," and the woman said, loudly and firmly without looking up, "DID YOU READ THE INSTRUCTIONS ON THE COUNTER," referring, it appeared, to laminated instructions on the counter. Billie tried to calm herself enough to read the instructions, which were confusing to both her and Gary. They had to take their forms, they finally worked out, attach their licenses to the forms, take a pager, and put the pager number on the form. They then had to take the pager back to the car and wait in the car. Two minutes after they had gotten in the car, the pager went off. When they came back into the building, they put their shoes and belts in a bucket and the same woman told them, with the same level of exasperation, that they had failed to fill out the time on their forms. The line just said "Time." Billie didn't know if it was supposed to be the time they'd arrived or the time it was when they filled out the form. She'd put her watch in the bucket. Phones weren't allowed. How was she supposed to know the time?

A security door opened, and everyone walked through to another room. Another security guard shone a light on Billie's wrist. Something was wrong; the other security guard had failed to mark Billie with invisible ink. They went back to her. A security guard opened a door and there were all the visitors and the people they had come to see, eighty people gathered around tables. Reality was not in the room. There were children's toys and games piled in the corner. There was a desk with two guards. “We are waiting for Reality,” Billie said to the guard. “WE KNOW,” he said sharply. Once again, Billie despaired. It was 9:20, two hours after they had left the hotel. Was there some new problem now?

When they came back the next time, and the next, Billie would stop and help anyone who looked confused, standing there with their forms at the table. She would patiently and kindly explain the process to new people; you clip your license here; don’t forget to note the pager number. She would explain that everything they had read in the rules was untrue. Nobody here even knew anything about the “fifth number of your registration” and even and odd days. That wasn’t how it worked at all. You didn’t have to have exactly six dollars in quarters. Eventually Billie, feeling helpless to improve conditions for her daughter and having retired from her job with social services, would get a full-time job as a guard in a prison near her home. That way, she could at least show some people the kind of kindness she wished the guards would show Reality. Reality would hate that her mother was putting herself through this, grow angry, scream into the phone, even stop speaking to her for a while. The intensity of their love would frequently overwhelm both of them.

When Reality walked in, she looked, to Billie, beautiful. She had cut her own hair and layered it nicely and had been able to use a flat iron for the first time in years. Here at the prison they could buy foundation and mascara. Across the room, Reality could see in her mother’s eyes a kind of ragged terror, everything she had been through to get to this moment. Reality started to cry. Billie started to cry. Gary too. Reality and Billie held one another and wept. Reality counted: *One. Two. Three.* They separated. Touching was allowed only at the beginning and the end of the visit. That rule was real.

It was a wonderful visit, everything for which Billie had allowed herself to hope. Billie kept thinking it would end, fearing it, but they were together for five leisurely hours. When Reality laughed her layers moved and she looked healthy and well and it was possible to believe she would come out of this okay. She would be able to buy running shoes at the commissary and run every day. There was the possibility of taking college classes. There was even a little area where they could visit with one another outside, and she and Reality and Gary sat in the sun and looked at pictures of their dogs. They sat so close together on the little bench under the sun and every so often Billie had the urge to touch her daughter's thigh or shoulder or squeeze her hand, but every time she looked up, the roaming eyes of a guard threatened to pass over her, so she kept her hands in her lap and she tried to be grateful.

ACKNOWLEDGMENTS

This book was made possible by Madison Allen, who watched my children with such extraordinary love and competence that I was able to think, for a few hours every day, about something else entirely. Thank you to Billie Winner for speaking to me against the advice of any number of lawyers, and to Brittany, for allowing me in. Thank you to wise Inara Verzemnieks for telling me I would write when I was ready.

Thank you to all the editors who have given me space to be strange, in particular Nick Gillespie, Chris Lehmann, Chris Suellentrop, and David Wallace-Wells. Thank you to John D'Agata for his mentorship, friendship, and for bringing me to Iowa, where a certain melancholic quiet made writing possible. Thank you to the faculty of the Nonfiction Writing Program and to the faculty of the Department of English at the University of Iowa, in particular Claire Fox and Brooks Landon. Thank you to the Andrews who made a public object of a Google doc: my agent Andrew Wylie and editor Andrew Miller. Thank you to everyone at Knopf, most especially Maris Dyer. I am indebted to Lei Wang for both early research assistance and late feedback, and to Gabriela Tully Claymore for her patient good-natured pursuit of absurd details, though the reader should blame me and not her for any facts that remain unchecked. Kalpana Narayanan patiently read many drafts of many chapters for years, and this book would not be this book without her insight or companionship. Thank you to Rachel Yoder for almost never asking about this manuscript while being so much of my world outside of it, and also to my fellow writers Kristen Radtke, Ariel Lewiton, and Zaina Arafat for their chorus of gossip and celebration. Lisa Ling, Daniel Hale, and Cian Westmoreland spent a lot of time helping me understand things I would not otherwise have understood. Thank you to Keith Golden for his dual role as source and inspiration. I am grateful to all of my colleagues at *New York* magazine for setting standards intimidatingly high, in particular David Haskell and Genevieve Smith. Thank you to Laura Poitras for her moral clarity. Thank you to Amanda Phillips for being my partner in crime and Sarah Viren for her steely lens. I am indebted to many people who do not wish to be named. They know who they are; I remain deeply grateful for their trust and time.

The first page of this book was written in Marfa, Texas, with support from the Lannan Foundation. The last was written in Oxford, Iowa, with the support of the Land Alliance Folk School and Retreat Center. Thank you most of all to William Wilkinson for supporting this project in myriad ways, and to our children, Fox and Tavi. May you be only as remembered as you wish.

BIBLIOGRAPHY

Berger, J. M. *Jihad Joe: Americans Who Go to War in the Name of Islam.* Lincoln: Potomac Books, 2011.

Blum, Andrew. *Tubes: A Journey to the Center of the Internet.* New York: HarperCollins, 2019.

Boyle, Michael J. *The Drone Age: How Drone Technology Will Change War and Peace.* New York: Oxford University Press, 2020.

Busch, Akiko. *How to Disappear: Notes on Invisibility in a Time of Transparency.* London: Penguin, 2019.

Cooley, Charles H. *Human Nature and the Social Order.* 1902.

Engelhardt, Tom. *Shadow Government: Surveillance, Secret Wars, and a Global Security State in a Single-Superpower World.* Chicago: Haymarket Books, 2014.

Gellman, Barton. *Dark Mirror: Edward Snowden and the American Surveillance State.* New York: Penguin, 2020.

Graff, Garrett M. *The Threat Matrix: Inside Robert Mueller's FBI and the War on Global Terror.* New York: Little, Brown, 2011.

Graham, Jorie. *Fast: Poems.* New York: Ecco, 2018.

———. *Runaway: New Poems.* New York: HarperCollins, 2020.

Gusterson, Hugh. *Drone: Remote Control Warfare.* Cambridge: MIT Press, 2017.

Harris, Shane. *The Watchers: The Rise of America's Surveillance State.* New York: Penguin, 2010.

Howley, Kevin. *Drones: Media Discourse and the Public Imagination.* Bern: Peter Lang, International Academic Publishers, 2017.

Isikoff, Michael, and David Corn. *Russian Roulette: The Inside Story of Putin's War on America and the Election of Donald Trump.* New York: Twelve, 2018.

Kiriakou, John. *Doing Time Like a Spy*. Los Angeles: Rare Bird Books, 2017.

——. *The Reluctant Spy*. New York: Bantam, 2010.

Kukis, Mark. *My Heart Became Attached: The Strange Journey of John Walker Lindh*. Lincoln: Potomac Books, 2008.

Leigh, David, and Luke Harding. *WikiLeaks: Inside Julian Assange's War on Secrecy*. New York: Public Affairs, 2011.

Lyon, David. *The Culture of Surveillance: Watching as a Way of Life*. Hoboken: John Wiley & Sons, 2018.

Mader, Chase. *The Passion of Bradley Manning*. New York: Verso Books, 2013.

Mayer, Jane. *The Dark Side: The Inside Story of How the War on Terror Turned into a War on American Ideals*. New York: Anchor, 2009.

Michel, Arthur H. *Eyes in the Sky: The Secret Rise of Gorgon Stare and How It Will Watch Us All*. New York: HarperCollins, 2019.

Mudd, Philip. *Black Site: The CIA in the Post-9/11 World*. New York: Liveright Publishing, 2019.

Pozen, David. "The Leaky Leviathan: Why the Government Condemns and Condones Unlawful Disclosures of Information." *Harvard Law Review* 127, no. 2 (December 2013).

Priest, Dana, and William Arkin. *Top Secret America: The Rise of the New American Security State*. New York: Little, Brown, 2011.

Radack, Jesselyn. *Traitor: The Whistleblower and the American Taliban*. Whistleblower Press, 2012.

Ridker, Andrew. *Privacy Policy: The Anthology of Surveillance Poetics*. Boston: Black Ocean, 2014.

Risen, James. *Pay Any Price: Greed, Power, and Endless War*. Boston: Houghton Mifflin Harcourt, 2014.

Romero, Anthony D. *In Defense of Our America*. New York: William Morrow, 2007.

Rosen, Jeffrey. *The Unwanted Gaze: The Destruction of Privacy in America*. New York: Vintage, 2011.

Scahill, Jeremy, and the staff of *The Intercept*. *The Assassination Complex: Inside the Government's Secret Drone Warfare Program*. New York: Simon & Schuster, 2017.

Shorrock, Tim. *Spies for Hire: The Secret World of Intelligence Outsourcing*. New York: Simon & Schuster, 2008.

Stanton, Doug. *Horse Soldiers: The Extraordinary Story of a Band of*

Special Forces Who Rode to Victory in Afghanistan. New York: Scribner, 2009.

Stephens, Paul. *The Poetics of Information Overload: From Gertrude Stein to Conceptual Writing*. Minneapolis: University of Minnesota Press, 2015.

Tucker, David. *The End of Intelligence: Espionage and State Power in the Information Age*. Redwood City: Stanford University Press, 2014.

United States & Feinstein, D. (2014). *Report of the Senate Select Committee on Intelligence: Committee Study of the Central Intelligence Agency's Detention and Interrogation Program*.

Zuboff, Shoshana. *The Age of Surveillance Capitalism: The Fight for a Human Future at the New Frontier of Power*. New York: Public Affairs, 2019.

A NOTE ABOUT THE AUTHOR

Kerry Howley is a feature writer at *New York* magazine and the author of *Thrown,* a *New York Times* Editors' Choice and pick for best-of-the-year lists in *Time, Salon, Slate,* and many other venues. Her work has appeared in *The Paris Review, Granta, Best American Sportswriting, The New York Times Magazine,* and *Harper's Magazine.* A Lannan Foundation Fellow, she holds an MFA from the University of Iowa, where she was an assistant professor at the celebrated Nonfiction Writing Program until joining *New York.* She lives in Los Angeles.

A NOTE ON THE TYPE

This book was set in Chronicle Text, a typeface designed by Hoefler & Frere-Jones in 2002. It is a Scotch face, created to withstand the effects of newspaper printing, in which low-quality paper and rapid printing speeds often caused delicate hairlines and serifs to disappear and enclosed spaces to become ink traps. Chronicle Text is offered in four press-sensitive "grades" to cope with these various printing challenges and works well in different kinds of media.

Typeset by Scribe, Philadelphia, Pennsylvania

Printed and bound by Lakeside Book Company, Harrisonburg, Virginia

Designed by Maggie Hinders

Grateful acknowledgment is made to HarperCollins Publishers for permission to reprint an excerpt from "Overheard in the Herd," from *Runaway* by Jorie Graham. Copyright © 2020 by Jorie Graham. Reprinted by permission of HarperCollins Publishers.

Small portions of this work first appeared, in slightly different form, in *New York* magazine.